Praise for
Open to Love

"I will buy copies of Dr. Gloria Horsely and Dr. Frank Powers's fantastic new book, *Open to Love: The Secrets of Senior Dating,* for over a dozen beloved family members, friends and clients. It's a must read!"

—Ken Druck, Ph.D., best-selling author, *Courageous Aging: Your Best Years Ever Reimagined* and *How We Go On: Self-Compassion, Courage and Gratitude on the Path Forward*

"Gloria Horsley and Frank Powers have written a unique book, *Open to Love: The Secrets of Senior Dating.* It's filled with the information that seniors in the dating world need. These two are an example of finding love again late in life and are an inspiration to those who may mistakenly believe that all the best is behind them. There is so much more adventure, laughter, and love to experience for those who dare to risk it."

—Linda Bloom, coauthor of *An End to Arguing: 101 Valuable Lessons for All Relationships*

"No secrets here. In *Open to Love,* Gloria and Frank reveal their story of finding love as seniors and provide a blueprint for others to find love for themselves. The pages are full of heart-warming and thought-provoking ups, downs, and all-around of how to be successful in finding love in the next chapter of your life, regardless of age. It's a practical guide leaving no room for the readers to say no to the idea of trying."

—Rachel Kodanaz
author of *Living with Loss, One Day at a Time* and *Finding Peace, One Piece at a Time: What to Do with Yours or a Loved One's Possessions*

"*Open to Love* is what everyone desires at any age. Those who experience it are the fortunate ones who enjoy it the most. May you be most fortunate!"

—C. Norman Shealy, MD, PhD

"Grounding their writing in decades of counseling clients facing relational transitions and drawing deeply on their own experience in launching a new life as a couple in their later years, authors Gloria Horsley and Frank Powers bring welcome encouragement and practical support to other seniors who are opening themselves to love following loss or disappointment. Their message is as hopeful as it is readable, with solid 'how to' advice illustrated with relatable anecdotes of their clients' struggles and successes, as well as their own. From confronting the anxiety of re-partnering through navigating the world of online matchmaking to exploring the risks and richness of new intimacy, this book serves as a wise and often humorous guide and companion. I'm already recommending it to others like myself who are seeking love that will last a lifetime—regardless of when they are initiating that search. To life!"

—Robert A. Neimeyer, PhD, director of the Portland Institute
for Loss and Transition and author of *Living Beyond Loss*

"Just having finished reading Gloria Horsley's and Frank Powers' wonderful new book, *Open to Love*, three words come to mind: It's about time. The authors are both psychologists and seniors themselves who found one another late in life after many personal losses. They've written a user friendly, positive, upbeat, and very hopeful guide for seniors considering entering the crazy world of twenty-first-century dating. If you are an elder with love in your heart and hoping to find love again, *Open to Love* is a must read."

—Robert Zucker, MA, FT, author of *The Journey Through Grief and Loss:
Helping Yourself and You Child When Grief Is Shared*

The Secrets of Senior Dating

Open
to
Love

Dr. Gloria Horsley & Dr. Frank Powers

Cover design by Mackenna Cotten
Cartoons and art by John Klossner

Open To Love song
Performed by Jill Colucci
Words & Music by Jill Colucci and Harold Payne
Producer: Jill Colucci
Executive Producers: Gloria Horsley and Frank Powers

Fedd Books
P.O. Box 341973
Austin, TX 78734

www.thefeddagency.com

Published in association with The Fedd Agency, Inc., a literary agency.

ISBN: 978-1957616575

LCCN: 2023922101

Printed in the United States of America

To Phil and his genius
that made all things possible.

Table of Contents

"IT IS UNCONDITIONAL LOVE,
BUT IT'S NOT ENOUGH."

Introduction

We are excited that you have taken the first step in your search for love. Adventure, fun, and companionship are waiting now that you're ready to take this journey, and we're here to be your guides. Writing a book was the last thing we thought we would be doing at this point in our lives (Gloria is 84 and Frank is 80), but some magical events brought this story about. We unexpectedly discovered the joys of being in a senior relationship, and we wanted to share them—and much more—with you.

When we started this project, even after years of working with thousands of couples, we were amazed at the lack of information for seniors about overcoming loneliness and experiencing the physical, emotional, and spiritual benefits of a loving, committed relationship. Dating today is so different, too—what are we to make of all the websites and apps we hear our kids or even our grandkids talking about? This book seeks to fill that void and provide the information you need to know to get out there and find love.

Throughout this book, you will sometimes hear the voices of both of us as a couple, and sometimes you'll hear from us individually. We'll start with our own stories of how this all came about.

 # GLORIA

In 2021, Phil, my partner of 60 years, died of a staph infection following back surgery. As I recovered from my grief, I began thinking about the years ahead of me. As a widow, I knew the statistics regarding spousal loss, so I figured Phil's death meant the end of romantic relationships for me and that I would likely be without a partner for the rest of my life. I felt like a statistic and not a happy one. I was now a part of the 80 percent of women who experience widowhood, and I knew the likelihood of finding a partner would get slimmer and slimmer over time. My prospects weren't looking very good. At age 70 there are 77.2 males to every 100 females and by the age of 85 that number drops to 55.2. I was 81 at the time. There would be a lot of competition for the few remaining eligible bachelors out there.

But then, six months after Phil died, I met a man in a grief group whose wife had died just two days after Phil. We shared a common interest in golf. This was during the time of COVID-19, and golf courses were one of the few places where masks were not required. We began a relationship, supporting each other through our ongoing grief and through the shared experience of our new companionship. Before long, though, my golfing partner made it clear that he thought we were not a good match after all. He had online dated and talked about it being a good way to meet potential partners. He told me his intention was to go find another partner, something he thought he would do "very quickly." (Hmm. Okay. I wonder how that went for him.)

In order to make sense of my life after the loss of yet another relationship, I decided to write a book for widows. I hoped this would help me sort through my feelings and experiences, and I wanted to share what I had learned in the senior dating world. There was so much that I had not been prepared for, including the lack of frank conversations about sex, money, and so many other parts of life. I felt that I had dived in blindly without really considering what my wants and needs truly were, and I thought a book would help me to figure those out for myself while encouraging others not to make the same mistakes. And if I was going to do this correctly, I'd need to write a chapter about online dating. I signed up for Silver Singles, a dating site for people over 50, for research. But as fate would have it, I met a new partner and widowhood became a book on "Finding The One." I sometimes like to kid around about the fact that I failed at Widowhood 101 and surprisingly moved on to Finding Love 102.

Getting back to my widow book, my first date was in Scottsdale, Arizona for a drink. The date was a nice eighty-seven-year-old man wearing a Shriner's shirt with "Dave" embroidered on the front. Dave spent most of the hour telling me how he had lost his memory after a year-long recovery from surgery for pancreatic cancer. He was a nice dude, but I wasn't ready to cope with his illness.

The second date was with my co-author and now-partner, Frank Powers. Like me, Frank had spent many years working as a psychologist. He was also a sculptor. He was quite amused when I explained to him that I was writing a book on widowhood with another psychologist friend and not really looking for a relationship. We connected immediately, though, and quickly found we had many common interests.

It wasn't just our interests that brought us together, but deeper shared experiences also. The same year Phil died, Frank lost his aunt, who was like a second mother to him, to lung cancer. We had also suffered other losses in our lives. When Frank was 15, his father had died following a sudden heart attack. My own son, Scott, had died in an automobile accident at the age of 17. We shared these stories and more over a series of dates, coming closer and closer together.

Today we are forging a wonderful and rewarding relationship, much like the one we wish for all of you who are looking for companionship and love. Together, Frank and I wrote this book so we could share our professional and personal experiences and guide you through the joys and challenges of senior dating.

FRANK

My story begins with some history: I have been married several times and have had other serious, long-term relationships. My story is different from Gloria's but what we had in common were losses. A year before I met Gloria I lost my aunt to cancer—she was my second mother and my close friend. I had an "almost relationship" (we'll explain this later) that ended just months before my aunt passed away. I was really lonely, and I reached out online.

This wasn't my first experience with online dating. During previous bouts of singlehood, I'd tried my luck on the internet, with mixed results—which I now think of as educational experiences. Three of my most meaningful relationships were the products of online dating. I felt that I was a seasoned veteran of the dating wars and was ready to take on all comers. So, it was a real surprise to this hardened vet to meet and fall in love with someone who took my breath away from our very first meeting. It's not exactly what I was expecting, but I was ready for it. By then, I knew what I needed—and, perhaps more importantly, what I didn't need—to heal my loneliness.

In this book, Gloria and I have had a wonderful experience manifesting our relationship. We both have learned so much in the year that we have been together. As therapists who regularly hear from others about the fears of "getting out there," we were surprised to see the lack of information and hope for seniors who are alone and lonely. With our own success, Gloria and I wanted to share our story and what we've learned as therapists in helping people who find themselves in the same situation.

We recently celebrated our one-year anniversary at the same restaurant in Scottsdale where we first met after connecting online. It was really the first time that we sat down and went over what had been going on in our heads at that initial meet-up. It was so much fun to revisit that wonderful time. Without asking, we were given the same table. We told the waitress about our experience and at the end of lunch she brought out a brownie with ice cream and a candle on top. It was as magical as our first date.

What this book offers

Part One: Getting Ready will help develop the skills and emotional readiness to date again in your senior years. Things have changed a lot since we all started dating, which for some of us might have been when Lyndon Johnson was in the White House and a gallon of milk cost 36 cents. Part One is to dating what spring training is to baseball: a time to brush up on the fundamentals and get ready. We want you to reexamine yourself, to be fully aware that you have what it takes to play. Through these chapters, readers will get to know their strengths and weaknesses, what they need and want to get out of the dating game, and what they need from a potential life partner.

Part Two: Senior Dating will take you through the entire process of dating, with an emphasis on the online world, where most of the action can be found these days. We cover everything from selecting an app to setting up a profile to all that happens afterward. We also discuss the pros and cons of the online world and its ability to connect people who would not normally meet in everyday life. We present the skills needed to get the most out of an online experience, and we teach readers how to deal with the everyday challenges that come with it. We know how to spot the scammers and how to handle the "almost experience," which we define as thinking that someone has found the love of their future, only to discover that it falls short. We discuss how to press on in the search for what might be the last love you'll ever need, and then we go beyond dating and through the four stages of a relationship. To conclude this section, we include a chapter to support those who find themselves facing or healing from break-ups.

Part Three: Relationship Challenges takes an unflinching look at the many factors that can cause duress. We discuss not only challenges but provide guidance for how to best navigate them, and we dedicate a chapter to previous losses and the grieving process, which can hamper the search for love. We provide tools to help assess where you are in the grieving process and discuss ways to keep moving through it. We conclude the book with a discussion of post-traumatic growth—the transformation awaiting us when we have endured and learned from our challenges.

Our overall wish is for readers to experience what we have experienced with each other. With the information in this book, we hope that you, too, will find a magical relationship that will last for the rest of your life.

Consider: am I looking for a soulmate, a friend, or a hook-up? One of the great asynchronies in dating arises because, in our experience, men and women often answer this question differently. We find that women tend to seek companions who can be a friend and a soulmate. Men, particularly those who have not changed their sexual attitudes since they were in their twenties or thirties, may have trouble attracting a loving, committed relationship. To further complicate this issue, these men are rarely straightforward in announcing their preferences. They'll claim they want a companion for life, but their actions and decisions will reveal that they're often looking for a sexual playmate—or even a mommy.

FRANK

Listen up! If a man did not grow up in a family where his parents modeled a loving and equitable relationship where tasks were shared, he could have no idea how immature and outdated his attitudes toward gender roles might be. In my experience of counseling men, I have found that this is the single most problematic area when it comes to preparing them for a deeper relationship. I've done more work here than anywhere else!

Senior daters in particular need to be on the lookout for underdeveloped adults, and to know they are not good candidates for a lasting relationship. They don't come clearly labeled, unfortunately, but one way you can tell is if they seem to struggle to take their eyes off of other prospective partners. These "bird dogs" often push too quickly for a sexual relationship, since that's their real motivation. Other signs of immaturity can arise in conversations about domestic expectations. Does a suitor want you to wash their socks, do their laundry, and to clean up after them? Such men are looking to have you take over where Mommy left off. Know what you're getting into!

Men, take a hard look at yourselves and ask if any of these descriptions apply to you. Do your attitudes match your age? If not, then you could have a hard time finding the relationship you're looking for at this point in your life. It isn't too late to change, though. If you're not sure how to make this change yourself, you may want to consider counseling. Once you identify and shift your focus to this issue, it usually doesn't take a long time to come around and prepare for senior dating. Take a tip from the man I'll call "Robert." (In this book, names have been changed to protect privacy.)

Robert was married three times before the age of 45. He came to counseling after his final divorce and was beginning to think that there must be something to his ex-wives' assertions. All three had similar comments about him: one, that he treated them like they were his mother, and two, that he only wanted them for sexual release when it was convenient for him.

Like his father, Robert grew up with the belief that if he "provided well" for his wife and family, he was "entitled" to be taken care of when he returned home from work. In compensation for his hard work, he should be given sex, clean shirts, and hot meals "on demand." Through the course of therapy, he came to realize that his attitudes and expectations were a major factor in his divorces. Because he considered himself a "three-time loser," he was ready and motivated to break free of the poor relationship model he'd learned from his father. He recognized that if he wanted his needs met, he had to address the needs of his partner. He joked about his old "golden rule" of dating: "Do others before they do you." It did not take long for him to understand why this approach had been a failure and to dedicate himself to changing his attitude and behavior.

GLORIA

Attractiveness

Attraction is a powerful and mysterious phenomenon. I was always puzzled by the beautiful movie star Sophia Loren who married Carlo Ponti. While Mr. Ponti was a great producer and filmmaker, he was 5'5" to his wife's 5'9", and I don't think it will be a controversial statement to say that she was far more physically attractive than he was. But Ms. Loren was seen with him at all the major film events of the fifties, clearly in love with him. Whatever it was she wanted, she knew what it was, and she found it.

So, consider: what do you want regarding attractiveness? Is height important? One of my clients, Sharon, won't date anyone who is less than six feet tall, as she doesn't feel comfortable being taller than her date. Mary Ruth, another of my clients, announced that she disliked beards and mustaches and would only consider clean-shaven dates. While we agree that physical attraction is important, we also suggest that clients don't give up on a potential partner due to looks alone. As the story of Sophia Loren illustrates, love might not look just the way we expect.

Physical appearance is very often an indication of good health, but it means different things at different times in life. When we're in our twenties and thirties, it suggests we will have healthy, attractive children. At our age, we look at attractiveness more as an indicator of health and hope for assurance that our partner will be around for a while.

The stage is set, and Part One of our book is next. Let's get ready to date!

"SORRY. I'M LOOKING FOR SOMEONE WHO CAN COOK."

PART ONE

Getting
Ready

"I'M LOOKING FOR SOMEONE WHO'S GENEROUS, WARM, FUNNY, PHILANTHROPIC, POLITICALLY ACTIVE, A FAMILY MAN, EMPATHETIC, HONEST — WITH A CONVERTIBLE."

CHAPTER ONE

The Perfect Partner

Welcome to the first step in the journey of senior dating! Some readers might come to us as a result of divorce, death, or a failed relationship or two. They might be at a point where their confidence has taken a hit; if so, this process can seem a bit daunting.

After decades of work as therapists with thousands of clients, we are here to tell you that you are stronger and wiser than you think. We've seen it over and over. Our clients often come in a bit bruised and battered, but on a deeper level, they're full of experience and knowledge. Tapping into this knowledge and making a change takes courage, but we know they are up to it. And as we can personally attest: love is well worth the time, the risk, and the energy expended.

We have all had our own losses and failures and we know how they can strike fear in our hearts. Perhaps we've chosen people who didn't meet our needs or put our faith in people who didn't deserve it. We have perhaps allowed ourselves to be abused and to be treated with shaming criticism. Many of us have also let people take advantage of our giving spirits and we've suffered feelings of abandonment. We've made mistakes, sometimes repeatedly. Some of those we've recovered from, but others we're still working through.

Even though we're both therapists, with 80 years of professional experience between us, we can't tell you what is best for you. Only you know what makes you happy. Only you know what you want, what you need. We can say with confidence, though, that if you're reading this, you've probably been through a lot. You've overcome many hurdles and in the course of all that, you've learned many lessons, whether you realize it or not. We believe that as a senior, you have within you the life experience and the skills necessary to find a loving and caring companion and to develop a beautiful, lasting relationship.

The first step to take in the dating process is to begin to identify needs and wants in a partner and a soulmate. Don't forget that trying new things can be fun and sometimes even funny. Try to keep a sense of humor! We will be with our readers, cheering them on throughout this book, and giving advice and examples from our own experiences.

What are you looking for in a partner?

The first step is to get a clear idea of what you're looking for in a partner. Without clarity, dating is like an employer deciding to hire at random without a job description. Just as we need pilots flying planes and actual surgeons in the operating rooms, we need a description of what is required in a partnership to guide us. What follows is a list of the major areas of compatibility we've come across in our careers as therapists. Give them a read and tune in to your feelings about each one.

1. Attractiveness
2. Emotional intimacy and sexual compatibility
3. Communication styles
4. Personality type
5. Religious and political views
6. Activities and interests
7. Honesty and openness
8. Family involvement
9. Money management
10. Domestic roles
11. Gender roles: caregiving, finances, and home maintenance

Don't think about casting a wide net; think of this instead as designing the perfect partner.

1. Attractiveness

This is often an indicator of how long people are going to be around. As we've all noticed, some people age much better than others. Because attractiveness often equates to health, assessments in this department can say something about how likely it is that one partner might become a caretaker, a widow, or a widower.

There's also the question of physical intimacy, of course. There's no escaping the changes that befall the bodies of older adults; being naked with each other at an older age is a challenge for many. Those who accept the changes in their own bodies usually have healthier attitudes about the changes taking place within their partners' bodies. Our mutual acceptance of our changes and our partners' changes is an important ingredient in a healthy relationship.

Nancy, a seventy-eight-year-old retired nurse who had been practicing yoga for decades, was having difficulty finding men her age who had taken equal care of their bodies. Most of the men who wanted to date her had a number of health problems. In counseling, she said that finding someone who matched her health level at her age was her number-one challenge in dating, and she decided to open herself up to the possibility of dating younger men in the hopes of finding someone who is as fit as she is.

It's important to remember, though, that this is not a perfect science. After his wife died, Fredrick, a minister, remarried a younger woman who was the organist in the church. He was hoping that her youth and attractiveness meant they'd have years together, and that she would have the energy to take care of him if he became ill. Unfortunately, she contracted stomach cancer soon after their marriage, and she died just two years after their wedding. His fear of being disabled came true when, a year after her death, he suffered a stroke. He now relies on his two daughters to care for him.

Frederick's experience is not typical, but it's a good reminder of the fallibility of our fortune-telling skills when we rely too much on youth and attractiveness to guide our decisions. The unforeseen can strike at any time. But health and energy levels are important factors when we're considering how compatible a potential partner might be. If one partner can't keep up with the other, it could have a significant impact on the amount of quality time available to the new couple.

FRANK

2. Emotional intimacy and sexual compatibility

Physical contact with other people is a basic human need. We've known this for decades, and it's supported by research from the fields of psychology and biology. When the system is working right, this begins in infancy, with mothers who are programmed to hold us while feeding and to soothe our cries with cuddles. As time goes by, our experiences and our maturity change the expression of this need, but it remains just as strong. As adults, intimacy and sexuality become key aspects of a healthy relationship, yet they are topics we often avoid in the early stages.

In our early conversations, Gloria and I shared that one of the things we did not like about being single and alone was the lack of physical contact. For Gloria, it went on for years due to her husband's multiple health issues; for me, it depended on whether I was currently in a relationship. Now that we're together, one of the things that we both enjoy the most is hugging, kissing, and cuddling. Because we both knew how we felt and what we wanted, we were able to speak to each other about this early and openly.

To have such a conversation, it sometimes helps to start by acknowledging that this is not our first relationship, and we have both learned a lot from life and living. This knowledge is priceless in getting everything we can in what is perhaps the last relationship in our lives. To do this, we need to share with one another what we have learned about what works for us and what does not. We need this so that we do not make the mistakes of the past and that we get in this relationship the caring and love that we have found to be important.

Our partners cannot read our minds. If they love us and want to please us, they need a roadmap that only we can provide one another. This has helped Gloria and me to be close to each other with less guesswork and the trepidation that comes with not knowing.

This sharing also affects longevity. Research shows us that married couples who know how to be emotionally and physically close live longer than single individuals who don't have regular sharing and human touch. As important as physical intimacy is, though, we all have varying needs. What one person might experience as everyday closeness and affection, another might perceive as unwanted or invasive. The following are some low-key questions that might help when talking about physical relationships:

- Where do you stand on intimacy?
- Are you looking for a lot of contact or a little contact?
- How much space do you like around yourself?

Sexual compatibility is a much more complex issue, especially for seniors. We have all had both good and bad sexual experiences that color how we approach physical intimacy in a new relationship. Later in this book, we devote a whole chapter to discussing this complex subject with the sensitivity and respect that it deserves.

FRANK

3. Communication styles

Being able to communicate effectively with a potential partner is critical. We each have our own styles: some people consider themselves to be strong, silent types while others like to be in frequent conversation, talking whenever and to whomever they can. Whatever the tendency, examine this trait in yourself and think about what style would work in a partner.

The distinction between introversion and extroversion is very helpful when considering this. I have long found valuable the work of Susan Cain, who wrote an excellent book called *Quiet: The Power of Introverts in a World that Can't Stop Talking*. Cain and other researchers who have studied introversion and extroversion describe this trait as one of the single biggest factors in determining the communication styles of most people. In her book, she addresses the differences between these styles and provides excellent resources to help you determine yours and your partner's. If you don't have a partner, her tools can also help you figure out what styles might complement yours.

As Cain indicates, extroverts and introverts are often drawn to each other, and seem to enjoy being with someone of the opposite style. The author herself is an introvert who is married to an extrovert, and Gloria and I have a similar dynamic. Knowing the style of a potential partner and understanding the differences in the way people communicate can go a long way toward facilitating conversation and creating a foundation of understanding.

Beyond these styles, the approach to sharing feelings is another major aspect in the communication between partners. Some people like to share their feelings about all sorts of things, but others do not. Since both Gloria and I have a long history as therapists, we tend to share to the nth degree—to the point that others might experience it as sharing *ad nauseum*. Partners will need to decide what, how, and how much sharing of feelings and past history feels right. Certainly, if partners have similar comfort levels, it will make their time together much easier and more enjoyable.

GLORIA

I really appreciate Frank's communication style. It is very gentle and caring. He is not only open to talking about my deceased husband, Phil, but he is also willing to have open, genuine conversations.

He shows compassion and interest when my family—three daughters and ten grandchildren—bring up their dad's or their grandpa's name.

Others are not so fortunate. I've seen how conflicting communication styles can cause marital strife and can play a large role in divorces and beyond. Such was the case with Rosemary and Donald. Donald was an extrovert who was very social and shared what was happening in the family with all of his friends, which made Rosemary very uncomfortable; she would have preferred much more privacy. Even after their divorce, the children complained to Rosemary about their dad telling other people embarrassing details of his and their life. Rosemary told them that she couldn't control their dad, but she did what she could to empower them to speak up for themselves and to tell him to stop when he was embarrassing them. She felt for her kids, but it was a relief to her personally that she was no longer responsible for trying to control her ex-husband's embarrassing tendencies. As her children grew into young adulthood, they figured out what to expect from their father and they developed their own ways of coping.

 GLORIA

4. Personality type

Another way to delve into communication styles and see what makes people tick is through an ancient system called the Enneagram, which divides people into nine different personality types. Frank is a Type Nine: The Mediator, and I am a Type Two: The Giver. We both agree that given our types we never would have gotten together early in our lives but with age our types became very compatible. Not that the Type Two and the Type Nine don't get together, but in our early years we both had ambitions of wanting to get out of cloistered environments (Frank out of Arizona and me out of Utah). In order to accomplish our desires for adventure we took very different routes.

I was a small-town girl looking to get out to the city, so was it any surprise that I fell in love with and married a fellow who was voted Most Likely to Succeed by his high school class? To my delight, we ended up living in New York City and New York State for many years. Frank, on the other hand, got out of Phoenix through the YMCA, whose adult leadership practically adopted him after his father died. He eventually was offered a fully paid scholarship to the YMCA's leadership university (George Williams College in Chicago).

Both Frank's type and my type like to help others achieve goals, and we don't like the pressure and obligation that can come with high-stress environments. Frank being a Type Nine is body-based, tends to be low-key, and values peace and harmony. He likes to measure his words and tends to be a bit cautious in his movement in the world—unless he is pushed. Then watch out! Type Nine is anger gone to sleep, and it's best not to wake a sleeping tiger. I, as the Type Two, am heart-based. When pushed, I can also go to anger, but Type Two is very forgiving.

Frank and I both merge with people, but Frank as a Type Nine, one-to-one guy. On the other hand, I, as a Type Two, am outgoing and work the whole room. As a young woman, I was attracted to males who were driven in life and business; Twos like to be the power behind the throne and not the leader. I wanted a big family and ended up having four children and a 60-year marriage. Frank, on the other hand, wanted to pursue his education and did not see having children as a priority. He enjoyed his bachelor life and a variety of relationships and marriages over the years.

You might ask what has brought us together now. I would say the biggest factors are commonalities as well as differences. We understand personality types and have unending conversations regarding our motivations. I like the Enneagram while Frank likes The Myers-Briggs Inventory and the work of Susan Cain regarding characteristics of introversion and extroversion, with Frank as the introvert and me as the sensitive extrovert.

We both enjoy the fact that we have been psychotherapists for many years and speak the same language. We are close to the same age and thus we share the same music, and we both love old movies. We both enjoy watching basketball and like swimming and playing sports such as pickleball and golf. Frank as a Type Nine tends to be more low-key than I am, which I like because he keeps me grounded. He enjoys the Type Two in me because I challenge him to try new things such as writing a book and doing podcasts. Since we are both semi-retired, we have a lot of freedom to travel and pursue activities that we both enjoy.

We do have differences and we have made a pact that if we do not want to do something, we can just say "no." This can include travel. I went to India a few months ago with my kids while Frank happily stayed home. Although at one time Frank had a fairly large family, today most of his close relatives have died and he is very much enjoying my family. Well, mostly enjoying—further on in the book we'll discuss how bringing a stranger into the family had its challenges. It does make it easier for me that he is an only child with two lovely stepdaughters and no biological children.

Another aspect of the Enneagram was taught to me by Dr. Helen Palmer, who wrote the first book published in the US on this system and its subtypes. While it can take time and study to understand the entire Enneagram system, a part that Frank and I found to be particularly useful when it comes to compatibility in dating are three subtypes. People tend to lean toward two of the three:

1. Sexual: This subtype likes a one-to-one relationship.
2. Social: This subtype enjoys being in groups.
3. Self-preservation: This subtype likes to stay home or have people come to their home.

The sexual subtype says, "Let's go out, just the two of us, and have a candlelight dinner." The social subtype says, "Let's invite a group of friends to go out." The self-preservation subtype says, "Let's stay home or invite people over."

While looking at the Enneagram subtypes, Frank and I have

noticed that couples struggle more if they don't connect on the subtypes that are most important to them. If you're someone who loves being out around groups of people, you're likely to get frustrated with someone who's reluctant to leave the house. We've seen that it can be particularly problematic if one partner is a sexual subtype and the other is not.

So, what are your subtypes and what you are hoping for in your partner? Make it a priority in the early stages to understand and use that information to be on the lookout for incompatibilities. I am a sexual, social subtype, while Frank is a sexual, self-preservation subtype. Sometimes we might disagree on whether to go out or order in, but in the end, it works for us because we are both sexual subtypes and like a lot of hugs and kisses.

For an easy, entertaining introduction to the Enneagram and its subtypes, we recommend *The Enneagram Made Easy*. Authors Elizabeth Wagele and Renee Baron explain the various personality types through the example of a dinner party.

5. Religious and political views

Although younger generations seem to be shifting their attitudes toward the importance of religion in their relationships, it's still important for many of us seniors. How strongly we feel about holiday celebrations, attendance at religious services, food restrictions, and belief in an afterlife are often important factors in compatibility.

 # GLORIA

Religion was an important factor in my childhood. I was raised Mormon, a religion which has a number of set restrictions and beliefs. One important restriction is that someone does not have an intimate relationship with someone unless they are married. Frank had no specific religious affiliation. I really had to think about breaking the rules I had grown up with.

Just prior to his death, my late husband talked about how I would go on to be with another man. I protested at the time, but looking back, I can now see that he was, in a sense, giving me permission. Giving myself permission was another matter. I had a candid discussion with my three daughters about my concerns about being a bad example to my ten grandchildren. The girls pointed out that half the grandchildren were already in relationships themselves and that I should do what would make me happy. After this discussion, Frank and I decided to move in together. It wasn't an easy decision, and I really had to give it a great deal of thought. Now, I'm happy to say that this has been a great choice for me, made possible because we were all able to openly discuss our beliefs and expectations while in the early stages of the relationship.

Other stories don't end quite so harmoniously. Jane, a sixty-five-year-old, came in to see me just after she'd retired from her career as an accountant. She had a strong Catholic background, and she'd met a Jewish man online. He met all of her requirements for age and interest in social activities, and they dated for several months. As time went on, though, she found that she just couldn't get comfortable with his family or their calendar of holidays and family rituals. She realized the deep importance of religious compatibility for her and finally decided to break off the relationship.

Political leanings can be even more divisive. The last decade has brought about some major political polarization, both worldwide and specifically here in the US, and this is becoming a bigger and bigger potential problem for people who are considering their dating choices. A number of our clients have indicated that they can't be interested in people whose politics are different from their own. Each person needs to decide where they stand on this issue, and they should be clear on which issues are deal-breakers.

One such client, Roberta, said that her partner liked to watch *Fox News*, which made her want to "throw up." She, on the other hand, liked to watch *The View*, which he felt was liberal male-bashing. They compromised by listening to music they both enjoyed when they were together. They weren't living in the same home so it wasn't a huge problem, but it was hard for her to imagine how things would go if the relationship were to progress and they were to move in together. When elections were on the horizon, she began to realize they were facing a major incompatibility.

Situations like Roberta's aren't uncommon. Whatever these deal-breaker issues are—religious, political, philosophical, or something else entirely—know where you stand, and honor your feelings. These differences may start out small but can grow and become roadblocks to continued closeness and intimacy. Frank and I have different religious backgrounds and slightly different political attitudes. These differences don't affect us much, as there are so many other attitudes, opinions, and beliefs that we share.

6. Activities and interests

Most people say that shared interests and activities are very important, especially at this point in our lives. We have fewer childcare responsibilities, fewer work demands, and most of us are not looking to launch a new endeavor, business or otherwise (although apparently some of us get together and decide to co-author books!). In the absence of time-consuming work and family obligations, we might turn to travel and leisure activities, and many of us are searching for a playmate to share the enjoyment. Others may have hobbies or ongoing work we like to pursue in solitude. It is important for each of us to decide how much play time we want with a partner and what activities we'd like to share.

Think about the activities that mean the most. Are you an avid traveler? If so, do you want someone who will happily join you on trips, or would you be content with someone who chooses to stay home and await your return? Perhaps you're a musician who spends time practicing an instrument or singing and performing. Is music a solitary pursuit, or would you like someone who can accompany you or provide a voice for a duet? How about cooking? If you've spent years practicing the culinary arts, would you like a sous chef, or at least someone with a refined enough palate to appreciate your skills? How about dating someone who's content with frozen pizza or boxed macaroni and cheese?

While such activities don't typically involve big philosophical clashes, incompatibilities can lead to disagreements about spending time in the relationship, and these can lead to resentment and dissatisfaction. Consider each other's lifestyles and how important those activities are, as well as how a potential partner might fit in.

FRANK

Gloria is a great golfer and has a passion for the sport. I played tennis in college and have a similar passion for the game, even though I've shifted to pickleball lately. We've embraced each other's sports; I'm now trying to keep up with Gloria on the golf course, and Gloria is learning to play pickleball. For younger people with less leisure time, compatibility around work schedules, child-rearing styles, and the like might be more important. But for those of us with more free time, activities like sports, music, travel, and hobbies typically take up a larger portion of our days. When choosing a future partner, don't downplay a desire for compatibility around the things you love to do!

Also, check in with yourself about how comfortable you are with a partner's needs to play with others (not just you). If a potential suitor has a longstanding golf foursome with buddies every

Saturday morning, will you be okay on your own during those hours every week? What if instead of a golf foursome, it's overnight camping trips? What about activities that you love doing solo—how will it feel if a partner asks you to give some of that up?

In our therapy offices, we've seen that there can be big differences in comfort levels here. Spend some time really figuring out where you stand, and when considering dating possibilities, ask where that potential partner stands as well. Make sure to sign up for a playmate who will meet on shared terms and play in your sandbox, whatever and wherever it may be.

While there's obviously much more that goes into long-term compatibility, shared interests like these can be ready icebreakers and an easy way to set up those early dates and to begin getting comfortable with each other. We recommend looking at this aspect of life and making a list of favorite activities and interests. Pay special attention to the ones you want to share with a partner.

We were fortunate to find common ground in several areas, which made those early days of our relationship exciting and full. In my family, we had a lot of fun playing cards with one another. Some of my favorite memories are of my family sitting around the card table, playing pinochle and hearts. It was a wonderful surprise to find out that Gloria's family has the same interest in cards. I would go so far as to say that it has been the single most important way that I have connected with her family. They are an amazing group of card sharks, and they've welcomed me right into their fold. Whenever possible, playing cards is her family's activity of choice, and this shared interest has really helped me to connect with them.

GLORIA

For some of us, sports have been a lifelong endeavor. In my dating profile, one thing I always made clear was that golf is an important part of my life. I even wrote that I wanted a partner with a handicap! It was a joke for the golfers, and when it confused someone, I knew he wasn't right for me.

If physical activity is important, then take a close look at each person of interest, because athletes and "couch potatoes" don't match well. Try to figure out what their actual activity levels are, beyond what they might list. It's easy for someone to click on an activity in a profile, particularly if they know it'll make them appear attractive, but there's a big difference between an avid hiker and someone who takes a short nature stroll every once in a while. After years of spending my weekends on golf courses, I can't tell you how many times I've seen men buy golf clubs for their girlfriends, who would quit the game once they got married. They might have been golfing, but they weren't golfers. Think about the overall role that sports or physical activities have played in your life and decide how important it is to find a compatible partner.

This extends to watching sports on television, too. For some, watching football can consume several nights during the season. This can also be said for golf, basketball, baseball, soccer, tennis, and any other sport that gets a lot of airtime. When considering a partner who likes to watch a lot of sports, if you're not into them, be prepared to do other activities, or invest in a second television and watch different things. The average US adult watches five hours of television a day, so there could be a big chunk of waking hours during which partners may or may not be compatible. If there are strong feelings about this one way or the other, make sure to include this in the process of selecting a partner.

7. Honesty and openness

While we all like to believe that the world is filled with honest people, we also believe that it is important to approach a potential dating relationship with a dose of skepticism. This doesn't mean being cynical—just pragmatic, and protective of one's own time and energy.

GLORIA

When I was growing up, I had a wealthy friend I'll call Susan, who was, she thought, an only child. Her father traveled a great deal and would be gone for weeks each month. She had everything but a present dad. After Susan left home for Smith College, her father announced that he was leaving her mother. After the divorce, Susan discovered that her father had a second family in another state.

Five years earlier, he had married and started living part-time with an airline stewardess he had met on his travels. Not only that, but Susan had three stepsiblings in addition to the stepmother she'd never known about.

In our careers as therapists, we've seen many other stories like this. Sometimes when we're seeing couples, one of the two will ask to also have a series of individual sessions. Often, it's because that person is having an affair or is carrying some other dark secret and wants us to take care of their partner. We've learned to refer them to a different therapist for those individual sessions, as it can quickly become a conflict of interest in couples' therapy.

Dishonesty and the resulting lack of trust are probably the biggest relationship-killers out there, so openness and honesty should be job number one in coming together and building a shared life. The resulting trust will be the foundation for a committed, honest relationship.

8. Family involvement

When thinking about committing to a relationship, it is important to consider where and how both people will interact with each other's families. There's a reason why so many comedians have joked about in-laws over the decades. Incompatibilities with family relationships can put great strain on relationships and introduce all sorts of conflict. Just ask Romeo and Juliet!

Take a look at your life. What are the expectations in your family? Are you used to spending holidays and vacations with relatives? Do you talk daily or take walks or have lunch often with family?

Take a moment to calculate how much time you spend with family yearly and ask if you would be willing to share this time with a new partner, as well as how much time would you be willing to give up for a *partner's* family. Would it be okay if you travelled or vacationed with families *on your own*? Would you even want to go without your partner? Would they want to come?

The only way to know is to ask. Ask each person of interest how much time they would be willing to spend with your family, and about their expectations for your use of time. The answers should not be set in stone. We all change our minds and have the right to do so. Leave room for negotiation as there are a lot of unknowns in a new relationship.

 **GLORIA**

In my experience with Frank, family involvement is not a big issue as he is an only child, has no biological children (he has two stepdaughters), and no close relatives. Things are a little different on my side of the equation. I have a big crew, with kids, grandkids, in-laws—you name it. Before I met Frank, I was dating a man who packed up and headed for the hills after a Christmas vacation with my 23 relatives. That was fine with me. My family is close, and if you can't handle them, you're not the right guy for me.

Frank negotiated my clan with much more success and grace,

but as we mentioned, he's a self-preservation subtype in the Enneagram, which means he likes his time and space. I really appreciate his ability to say, "No, thank you," and retire with a good book. In doing so, he's taking care of himself, which I like—it's the mark of a man with emotional maturity. At the same time, though, we devote time to discussions to make sure his choices don't come across as rejections. These can be difficult conversations but avoiding them can lead to some pretty hard feelings.

Fran, age 40, came to therapy angry and sad not only because of the death of her father but over what she perceived as the loss of her mother to a new relationship. She broke into tears in my office over her mother's lack of availability once this new partner came into the picture. When her parents were both alive, they'd had a family tradition of renting a house on Cape Cod for the summer. With her dad's death, though, things changed. Her mom not only declined to rent the home and invite her and the family, but in fact, she opted to take what Fran called a "lavish vacation" with her new boyfriend's family. Fran and her children hadn't been invited.

I tried to get her to see and accept the inevitability of change. I pointed out that family involvement was obviously important to her mother's boyfriend, and that over time, this might include Fran's family. As this was a new romance and relationship, it would take time to blend the families. And while she might have less time with her mother, she might find a way to enjoy this new person coming into the family. Although the loss of her father was understandably difficult, my hope for her was that in time, she'd find a way to see her mom's boyfriend as a new family member.

With death and recoupling, there naturally comes what we call a "storming phase," which is a period of unpredictability and volatility, often marked by difficulty. (We'll cover this more fully in Chapter Six.) As with all things, it passes, but there are some ways to ride it out that are more graceful than others. After a divorce or a death, it can be wise to hang back for the first year or two and plan some fun things with those you currently care about, perhaps including some friends and family members you don't often see.

9. Money management

Another big aspect of senior dating is finding someone who is financially stable and won't be overly dependent, rather than someone who will drain your financial resources. Most often it's not about the actual amount of money each has. Instead, we have found that it is fiscal responsibility that matters most.

One of our clients, Sam, a dentist in his late sixties, met a woman online. She was very attractive and, at first, seemed financially stable, with only a small mortgage on her home. They married after six months and then two years later she took all the money out of the line of credit connected to *his* home. He found out from a relative of hers that this wasn't the first time she had done something like this; she had done the same thing in a previous marriage. He made the painful decision to terminate the relationship and successfully went after the bank for letting her drain the account.

Many problems like this don't work out so well, so do a thorough financial assessment before tangling your finances up with someone else's. And before planning a wedding, create a prenuptial agreement. Some may complain that a prenup takes the romance out of things but at this age, practicality and security are more important. For a responsible senior relationship, we believe that a prenup is essential. There are plenty of other departments where romance can flourish!

GLORIA

Consider gender roles when it comes to money management as well. We have found that many men of our generation handled the money and gave their wives a kind of allowance. It is not uncommon in our generation, then, to see big adjustments in a new relationship from the practices of our previous relationships. As our clients tell us, times are a-changin'. So, if you would like to see changes in the way money was managed from your last relationship to your next relationship, this is an excellent time to figure that out. As in the next example, what was tolerated in the past may not work today.

Mary, another client, thought it strange that when she freely shared the state of her finances, her boyfriend Kenny did not. He was very quiet and controlling. The only thing she knew was that Kenny had been an entrepreneur, but she didn't have any information on his income or his net worth. His lack of sharing impacted their relationship because she was reluctant to suggest nice restaurants or travel as she didn't know what he could afford. Mary and her late husband had traveled around the world on business, staying in top-rated hotels and flying first class. For her, those luxuries had become a big part of the pleasure of traveling. Kenny, though, felt that it was a waste to pay for anything but the economy class in both flights and hotels. Mary said that she missed sitting next to him on the plane, but she tried to respect his choice to fly economy. He agreed to stay in better hotels when she offered to pay three-quarters of the bill, but she could still sense his discontent at what he felt was a waste of money.

Kenny's insightful son, who was in favor of their relationship, pointed out to him that the difference could be related to gender. For generations, the earning expectations for men have been different than they have for women. So, if you're a woman and find you have more money than a potential partner, be prepared for some ego issues. As with the other issues in this list, early, open, and honest conversations are the way to head off conflict.

Does this mean you need to tell a potential partner all about your finances? Absolutely not. One of our friends who was a money manager had this piece of advice for single women: "Do not have brokerage, bank, or retirement statements sent to the house if you are single and dating. Keep things online." Sound advice, unless you know a great deal about the person you are dating. Before that point, it is best that they don't see financial documents. Don't leave things around the house or receive mail related to finances until you're very sure of the person you're dating.

It's possible to learn a lot about someone through services like TruthFinder, Check People, or eVerify, which enable users to search public documents, such as criminal and civil records. There's no violation of privacy here—these services simply collect public records from all the different sources where they can be tucked away, where normal search engines don't reach. And personal connections might help track down additional information.

A friend of mine has an in-law in the police department who is willing to help look through public court filings and other records that might reveal financial red flags. Another friend, Diane, was dating a doctor when a loved one helped her look into his records. She found out that the doctor had been divorced four times and had three bankruptcies. She also realized that her condo could be confiscated if she married him. She very sadly broke up with him, telling him she could not risk her financial future.

While it may be none of our business what a partner does with his or her money, we need to stand up for our own needs. Some people are stressed over money to the point where it interferes with their lives on a daily basis. On the other hand, there are people who have very little yet live in bounty, enjoying this beautiful world and all it has to offer. So, check in with yourself and your desires in a partner when it comes to finances. Look for someone who is fiscally responsible yet not overly worried about whether their money will run out before their body (so to speak).

FRANK

10. Domestic roles

I did my doctoral dissertation on "Domestic Role Changes in Dual-Career Couples." The study I conducted focused on couples who both had careers and looked at expectations that the wife should be a superwoman. Not surprisingly, such expectations don't work out very well. It's far too much to expect a woman who is part of a couple to have a successful career while also holding the primary responsibility for homemaking and childcare. I concluded that "domestic roles in these couples needed to be examined and needed to be divided equally between both individuals." I conducted this study a number of years ago, and I'm glad to see that the attitudes of younger adults seem to be taking this simple fact to heart, and that it has become better accepted.

Now, seniors need to learn a lesson from the younger generation. We can't just expect women to do the "traditional" chores all by themselves. At this point in our lives, domestic roles should be divided equally. If one loves to cook, the other should be prepared to do the dishes. If one partner has a green thumb, teach the other how to tend the garden. If there's a chore that neither wants to do, and the resources aren't available to hire someone else to do it, then both partners have to develop a fair way to decide who does it.

We're past the point of simply declaring that it's "women's work" or that it's "the man's job." Put those old stereotypes away and then engage with modern empowerment.

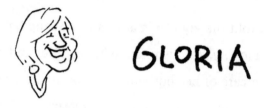

GLORIA

11. Gender roles: caregiving, finances, and home maintenance

I have heard so many single widows say (with a laugh) that they don't want to be "a nurse or a purse." But the fact is, there are both male and female "nurses," and if we are to be in a loving relationship in the last quarter of our lives, we will be taking care of one another.

We need to be smart about our caregiving, though, which means stepping back and considering the whole picture and all the available resources so you can also take care of yourself as well. Are there rehab units or family members who can help with care? Plan for what type of care is needed and decide who is best able to provide it. People will step forward if asked, but often *only* if asked. In my past career as a nurse practitioner, it was not unusual for me to see burnt-out caregivers die before the patients. This doesn't need to happen, though—there is plenty to do to avoid caretaker syndrome (more about that shortly).

With a senior relationship, we need to be clear about the level of care we will be willing to give a new partner. I shared with Frank how I had developed alopecia and lost my hair as a result of taking care of my husband four years prior to his death, at the time when he first developed a staph infection and was in the ICU for ten days. This alerted him to the fact that I was highly susceptible to caregiver burnout.

He then told me about his aunt and how he had seen her go from being a loving, kind woman to being bitter and angry as a result of taking care of her husband after he suffered cardiovascular issues. I also saw my mother decline after years of taking care of my dad, who suffered multiple strokes. In both cases, neither woman would consider bringing in healthcare professionals. Frank and I have both seen a number of clients in the past who had burnout, mostly women but also a few men.

While in the midst of writing this book, Frank was faced with a long-needed knee surgery. I had taken care of my husband through many health crises, with numerous surgeries and hospitalizations, and I wasn't eager to go back to that. In our research, we discovered that the first two weeks following knee surgery are very difficult and require heavy medication and help. As such, his impending surgery was somewhat concerning for both of us, as we were both afraid that caretaking could impact our relationship.

Frank, however, was willing to recover in a rehab unit. This was a big relief for me. As a registered nurse and a woman, I was afraid that he would feel that I was "abandoning" him if I didn't take care of him. I admitted all this to him, and he assured me that it was fine, and that having others care for him would protect our relationship. So, we agreed, but that wasn't the end of the conversation.

Frank's doctor informed him that with modern technology,

his surgery would be minimally invasive, an outpatient procedure. Frank would be able to go home right after surgery. The medical staff's assumption was that he'd be happy to be home and that I'd be happy to have him at home where I could take care of him. But because Frank and I both knew what we wanted and we'd talked about it in advance, we told the doctor that home care would not be the best option. He was a bit puzzled at first—I don't think this is something they hear much. But he agreed to do the surgery in a hospital rather than his clinic so that Frank could stay overnight and be eligible for a rehab unit. That wasn't the end either, though.

A month later, we went back in for his pre-op appointment to have a conversation with the physician's assistant, who was a very competent and nice woman. There had been some miscommunication, though, and she said that I could pick Frank up after surgery and take him home. When we told her that Frank would be recovering in a rehab unit, she went on to talk about how bad rehab units are, that the majority of patients recover at home, and that he would get better faster if I stepped up. Talk about a guilt trip! We knew what we wanted, though, and we were finally able to get her off her soapbox and assert that Frank was going to rehab. I felt that she was working on me as a woman because she thought I should take care of Frank. Frank and I had other ideas, though. In a new relationship, we do not believe that caretaking has to fall on the partner's shoulders.

Caregiver stress syndrome, also known as caregiver burnout, affects millions of people every year. A 2020 survey conducted by the National Alliance for Caregiving and the AARP Public Policy

Institute found that 40 percent of caregivers felt emotional stress, 20 percent felt financial stress, and 20 percent felt physical stress. Other symptoms of this disorder can include failing health, poorer diet, and increased mortality rates. Caretaking is a serious matter and should not be seen as an obligation.

The health field has not caught up, however. In our observations, we've seen that the health care system pushes caretaking on to senior partners. This is especially true of women—another outdated stereotype. We all remember "in sickness and in health" from our long-ago marriage vows, but at this point, consider approaching things a little differently. As seniors in a new, committed relationship, Frank and I don't feel that we need to be joined at the hip. Rather, we think of ourselves as parallel travelers through life.

Take a moment and respond below to the following questions:

- What are my expectations concerning my partner regarding caregiving?
- What do I see as the male role in caregiving?
- How do I see the female role in caregiving?
- Do I feel that my doctor and the rest of the medical system will support me?
- Do I think that my family will support my attitudes toward caregiving?

Next, we suggest discussing the following with your partner:

- Past history of healthcare giving
- Expectation of the partner regarding health issues

- Expectation of your involvement with medical appointment and treatments
- Attitudes toward rehabilitation and rehabilitation facilities

FRANK

Like women, men typically also have financial and domestic concerns, although they might look a little different on the surface. Many are afraid that they will just be a "credit card and a honey-do-er" in a new relationship. They are afraid that a new partner will be interested only in the money and status the man might bring. Some of them have told me in therapy that they've known women who wanted their financial support but weren't so interested in sharing time or activities. I have had other clients complain about relationships where their partners preferred to be with their female friends. One client complained that his new partner only wanted to play mahjong and eat bonbons while he had a "honey-do" list a mile long. We men often have delicate egos where women are concerned, and we don't like to be seen as a wallet or a mark. Nobody wants to be used and abused.

For all people, though, it's common to focus on our own perspectives, sometimes at the expense of others. And at this age, we often have many decades of experience in prioritizing our views, which typically form in our late teen years. It isn't easy at this stage in life to take that step outside ourselves and to try to understand and appreciate our partner's perspective, but it is an excellent time to try. Don't be afraid to ask potential partners what they value about you. Share any concerns about being treated as a source of funding or one of the maintenance staff. At the same time, remain open to the same questions coming from the other direction.

For these conversations to be productive, it's critical to know yourself and know what you really want, deep down. There's a lot of cultural conditioning to dig through here. As young men, we were likely trained to look for beauty. We were often looking for partners who were sex objects or who would give us status with our friends. Men of our generation were often trained to see this person as they saw their car: as a possession and a status symbol.

The fantasy that many men have now is that their new partner will be younger, slimmer, and the couple's social director. In that sense, many of us haven't outgrown our search for a status symbol. One of my clients told me, of his new partner, "I love going out with her and watching other men not be able to take their eyes off her. Let them eat their hearts out! She's mine."

Older men are especially vulnerable to this attitude. The mid-life-crisis male often looks for a younger woman who demonstrates to other men that he still "has it." This sometimes makes the man vulnerable to being used by *their partners*, who themselves feel used for their youth and beauty. As Oliver Hardy used to say: "What a fine kettle of fish you have gotten us into, Stan." This is a terrible place for a man and his partner to be.

Men who avoid this midlife trap are usually looking for something else: a real partner who is first his best friend and then his lover. Rather than the misguided status symbol of, for instance, a woman who's much younger, a partner closer to his age can be the answer to loneliness. A person of our own era—someone who's closer in age—can share mutual experiences of growing up and growing older. This is what May-December relationships might lack. A big age gap could mean we won't share the same references in terms of music, dances, movies, or cultural events. And our experiences of each decade will be different, sometimes even unrelatable, and this can make it quite challenging to reach the depth of connection that might more easily form with a person of our own era.

It will make a big difference in dating attempts if we can get past the desire for a status symbol. Instead, seek out a life partner to share life's fun and excitement. After seeing these choices play out in my therapy office, I can honestly say that those men who choose to date someone closer to their age generally come away much happier than the alternative. So, sit down and take a good hard look at yourself and what you want. Do you want a companion, or do you want other men to envy you? If it's the latter, then first—good for you for being honest. Next, reach out for support to help move past that desire, and to make decisions based more on emotional and spiritual compatibility than impressing friends. It'll make a big difference in your long-term happiness.

What traits have you been drawn to in the past?
After daydreaming and visualization about ideal compatibility,

let's take a look at how things have worked in the past. Harville Hendrix, a therapist who has written several books on love and relationships, teaches us that we are drawn to the familiar. We each have an unconscious profile from our childhood that influences our dating quest. He goes on to say that with each failed relationship, we become more conscious and can more maturely look at what qualities meet our needs.

Hendrix asks you to imagine being at a party where there are twenty people present whom you might be interested in meeting. Now imagine spending just two minutes in conversation with each of them. Perhaps you are drawn to some of the individuals and not others. Specifically, we'll be drawn to the personalities that match the characteristics of the caretakers who raised us, whether these characteristics are good or bad for us. It's all unconscious. If we had an alcoholic or abusive parent, we may be drawn to people who have substance abuse issues or a tendency toward the same. If we allow our negative unconscious choices to become more conscious, we usually make better choices.

In his book *Getting the Love You Want,* Hendrix suggests making a list of the characteristics we find repeatedly in the people we have dated or married. This list will likely mirror our caretakers' major characteristics, and these characteristics will drive our unconscious choices while dating. And we need to consciously decide if these qualities are actually good for us or not. If not, it's time to figure out how to select differently.

We suggest taking a moment to make a characteristics list. Now ask: how well is your unconscious doing? Is it aligned with what you consciously say you want? Is it attracting you to qualities that are good for you? If your choices have been good in the past and you chose the right individuals to date, live with, or marry, then you are in good shape. If dating choices in the past have been more problematic, then take a close look at what you have been drawn to and why. You may have a bit of work ahead to make sure your experiences and your consciousness have more of a hand in guiding future choices. Take comfort in the knowledge that at this age, you've got plenty of both experience and awareness to help turn things around.

Sylvia was in her mid-sixties when she came into my office to get help finding what she called a "love match." She talked of the drama and tension that had marked her marriage and her several failed attempts at cohabitating with boyfriends. According to Sylvia, her father had been the "King of Drama." While he was handsome and seemed to be friendly and thoughtful, underneath he was a real Don Juan. He called her his "Little Princess" but treated her mother like his housemaid. He was an alcoholic and many of the stories she told contained elements of emotional abuse.

Over time, Sylvia took a look at the elements shared by the men she had chosen. Not surprisingly, she discovered that the major commonality was that she was attracted to "bad boys." By that, she meant that almost all of the men in her life had the same *modus operandi* as her father, with tendencies towards being emotionally and even physically abusive. A couple of her boyfriends had alcohol and drug histories. With therapy, Sylvia began to connect her unconscious choices to her history with her father. Recognizing her historical patterns helped her to identify what she was drawn to, and when she returned to dating, she was able to identify red flags and use conscious decision-making to break her patterns.

James, another counseling client in his seventies, came in reporting "mommy issues." He'd noticed a pattern, and he told me he was drawn to women who were attracted to his money and who would eventually leave him for another man or opportunity. For him, this was a "mommy issue"—his own mother had left his family for another man when he was ten years old, and he never heard from her again. At first, it was hard for him to believe that he was attracted to the characteristics that had hurt so badly as a child. But he could not refute his experience, repeated over and over, of choosing women who would leave him. As with Sylvia, recognizing these unconscious, toxic family patterns helped James to choose a woman who could commit.

If you are resonating with Sylvia's or James's story, we wouldn't be surprised. This is a big part of our work, and we've seen countless times when clients have been amazed to find traits of their caretakers in their past poor choices of partners. Using your Hendrix characteristics list and life experiences will reveal what you are unconsciously drawn to and will help with being more conscious about future choices.

Wrap-up

We hope that this chapter was fun and informative. We've now explored the traits and characteristics you need and want in a relationship. You have no doubt added some additional areas of compatibility and have now covered the preliminary work of getting ready for senior dating. This provides an idea of what you want and are looking for, as well as an awareness of how to keep an eye on any unconscious tendencies during this process. If a track record of decision-making has worked against you, we suggest creating a conscious plan to build new and better patterns. If you're stumped about how to break out of those old patterns that weren't working, seek the help of a therapist to dig into things a bit more. It's okay to feel a little intimidated by the process but recognizing these differences and the desire to change means that you're already well on your way.

This is a lot to think about, and if we're just looking to have some fun and meet some people for a drink here or a meal there, we don't have to spend too much time figuring all this out. But if we're looking for real love—possibly our last real love—then we'll want to figure out these answers. We're in a position now to make a clear declaration about what we want in a partner. The unqualified need not apply.

Once we have a good idea of what we're looking for in a partner, we're halfway there. The other half of preparation is facing any fears about the process of looking for this great partner. The next chapter explores and addresses any lingering trepidation or fears that might be standing between you and true love. Consider the eight areas discussed in this chapter, which will be of great benefit when reflecting on what you are looking for in a partner.

Journal questions

Consider the 11 areas we've discussed in this chapter and take time to reflect on what you are looking for in a partner.

- Activities and interests: Picture a perfect day. Is it spent out with a group of friends, on the golf course, or staying inside watching movies?
- Attractiveness: Ask, "What do I want as far as attractiveness goes?"
- Communication styles: Pause and reflect on your communication style. Do you lean more toward introversion or extroversion?
- Domestic roles: Think about the division of labor in your past home. Who did the cooking and the cleaning? What kind of division of household chores and domestic roles do you want and expect from a partner?
- Emotional intimacy and sexual compatibility: What kind of intimacy are you looking for in a partner?
- Family involvement: What kind and how much involvement do you expect and want from your family and a partner's family?
- Honesty and openness: How important is it that your partner is forthcoming and does not keep secrets?

- Money management: What kind of relationship do you have with finances? Are you a spender, thrifty, or frugal? Do you like to spend money on vacations and big gifts, or do you get excited about finding deals? How has gender informed your view of finances?
- Nurse or purse; wallet or "honey-doer": What level of care are you willing to give to a partner?
- Personality type: What kind of personality traits do you desire in a partner that would make life fuller?
- Relationship type: What kind of relationship are you hoping for? A soulmate, a friend, or a hook-up?
- Religious and political views: How important is it that a partner share your political and religious views?

"WE BONDED OVER OUR MUTUAL
FEAR OF RELATIONSHIPS."

CHAPTER TWO

Facing Relationship Fears

In our years of working as therapists, we have found that a number of our single clients have suffered what we have termed "relationship fears." We've heard thousands of individual stories, each of them unique, but their core feelings of reluctance are similar. We've put together a list of the most common reasons we hear for staying home and steering clear of the dating world. Some of these might sound familiar.

We'll take each one in turn and share our responses, which come from the stories of our clients, friends, and family, as well as our own considerable personal experience. Our hope is that by first identifying such fears, readers will be able to address them and begin taking steps to overcome them. Sometimes this can be hard, even when we're motivated by loss and loneliness. Always remember that community and support are out there, whether from professionals like us or from others who have been through similar things and who have overcome similar fears.

Here is a list of 11 fears and concerns about dating that we've heard over and over from our clients:

1. What if I get hurt again?
2. My friends or family will be upset.
3. I'm not good dating material.
4. A scam artist will just take advantage of me!
5. A pet will be safer.
6. All the good people are already taken.
7. I feel I'm being disloyal to my deceased partner or spouse.
8. It's easier to stick with paid sex or pornography.
9. Seniors like me will just get sick and die—I don't want to be a caregiver!
10. Why be open to criticism?
11. What if I don't find the right person the first time? Breaking up is difficult—I'll be stuck!

Which of these apply to you? It might be one, two, or several. Make a mental note, and don't worry! We'll take each fear in turn. They can be addressed—we've helped our clients through them, time and time again.

1. What if I get hurt again?

Losing a relationship can cause great pain. And while our personal trainers might encourage us with platitudes like, "No pain, no gain," this doesn't quite work in the world of dating. Here, we can't simply forge ahead, knowing that our discomfort is only momentary and that we're making progress with each rep.

It may help here to connect with the alternative source of pain: the pain of loneliness. If you're reading these words, you're likely feeling some level of this. Perhaps it hits hardest when sitting alone in a restaurant, or when crawling into an empty bed. Connect with this feeling, and then compare it to the perceived pain of losing someone. Remember that this is just *perceived* pain. It's hypothetical. As with anxiety, this is a fear that something difficult *might* happen.

But it might not. You could find the love of your life. And you are in control of how far to take any possible connections.

Now ask which is greater: the pain of loneliness or the fear of what might happen if you date? If it's the pain of loneliness, and you're feeling unsettled without a partner, then you can prepare to meet another person with whom to share life.

This is not to downplay any anxiety. It's very real and we honor those feelings; yet consider this: we don't have to be 100 percent free of concerns before taking those first steps. In fact, you've already taken steps, even if all you've done is crack open this book for a few minutes while strolling through a bookstore or shopping online. Our goal with these chapters is to help overcome anxiety enough to take those first steps, each of which will bring you more comfort and confidence that you can succeed in finding "The One."

2. My friends or family will be upset.

We realize that upsetting friends and family is a big relationship fear, as it was for us. In many cases, it's an issue that can't be avoided, because we can't make everyone happy. At such times, we like to think of the advice Gloria got from her old boss, Robert Sproull, the past president of the University of Rochester: "If you believe in it, go for it. Not everyone is going to agree with you anyway."

There are many reasons, both conscious and unconscious, for friends or family to be resistant to an attempt to find someone. It could simply be that they don't want to share you with an "outsider." Children might fear losing their inheritances to the newcomer, or seeing you get hurt. One thing is certain: they will have opinions, spoken or unspoken, one way or the other. Some of them will support the idea and some will not. The best approach is to prepare for their attitudes and opinions and remember, they're well-intentioned (usually, we hope).

In our case, the resistance from Gloria's three daughters came like a tsunami. While we did anticipate a reaction, we had no idea it would be that strong, and we were nowhere near as prepared as we are encouraging you to be! It was a hard lesson, which we will tell you more about in Chapter Six.

Each person's challenges will undoubtedly be different; yet be prepared to find out that not everyone will think that this dating thing is a good idea. It's your life, though, and as we'll repeat throughout this book, only you can decide what's right for you. There are ways to have the conversation that will honor the intentions of everyone involved, most of all your own.

We weathered the storm with Gloria's daughters and through some difficult discussions we found common ground. We all came together. We believe that others will be able to do the same, but we suggest coming prepared with your most protective storm jacket. And if things get contentious, just realize that your loved ones are protective. Chances are they want you to be safe and they want you to remain available to them.

3. I'm not good dating material.

This thought is what the late psychologist Albert Ellis called "stinking thinking." Ellis helped people to identify irrational beliefs and negative thought patterns such as these. We all do some stinking thinking. Such was the case with Sandy.

Sandy had tried to find someone through friends and family and recounted a number of boring dates. She had almost given up and said that her standard poodle, Sara, was enough. When we introduced her to the idea of stinking thinking, it gave her a great laugh, but she also saw the wisdom in it. She came to realize that her attitude was merely a bad mental habit and had nothing to do with who she actually was, or what she could bring to a relationship.

We then helped her to join an online dating service where she had more than 20 matches in her first week on the site. She began going out on dates again, having fun, but also maintaining what she calls "control" of her social life. With the recognition of her thought patterns, she took her power back and put herself in charge.

4. A scam artist will just take advantage of me!

Unfortunately, because so many people are looking for a connection with someone, there are also people who are looking to take advantage of these situations. The best way to deal with this is to learn to be a "good consumer" in the dating marketplace and to approach interactions with potential dates with care. Once someone is of interest and they provide their name and other personal information, do some research.

Gloria and I used Google to look each other up. In our case, we both had websites that contained information about our professional backgrounds and interests. There are also services (such as *White Pages*) that will, for a fee, provide information from public sources about the person's arrest records, residences, family, past marriages, and other public information. News articles and social media websites can provide other preliminary pieces of information. One caution here is to make sure to follow up after encountering a dead end with the person's name. They may have changed their name for many reasons, some of them due to business or personal preference.

Don't feel guilty about internet research—it's not being sneaky or violating anyone's privacy! This isn't peering over someone's fence or eavesdropping on their personal conversations. This is just being smart, making sure you know what information is out there in the public domain. It is very important for safety's sake to know if the person is who they say they are. Similarly, encourage them to verify that you are who you say you are. Having them check you out makes it easier for you to make inquiries about them.

FRANK

Tom, a client in counseling, reported that he had met an interesting woman online who lived in another state. They struck up a lively conversation through texts and emails. Things seemed to be going along fine until she said that her mother had become ill and that she needed money to assist her. Tom became suspicious and with my encouragement, he checked her out. A thorough search for her name yielded no results, leaving him to conclude that she did not exist, and that this was indeed a scammer! I suggested he report this profile to the online service, and it was soon removed. Tom said the experience made him a better consumer of the service and he became determined to check people out earlier in the process.

Tom emerged pretty much unscathed, but we've seen people who are so blinded by "love" and the promise of companionship that they have avoided bad news about a potential partner. Such was the case with our friend Barbara, who lost her first husband through a divorce, and then a second one to a heart attack. After a couple of years, she signed up for an online service and then fell madly in love with a connection she'd made. Her new love was on a job assignment out of the country, though, so they would not be able to meet in person until he returned. Nevertheless, she felt she'd found the man of her dreams, and even went on to meet his kids online.

But then things took a turn. He told her he needed financial help. She started out by sending him small amounts of money, and then she sent a large sum to help him with travel back to the US. Her son tried to tell her that it was a scam, but she waved his concerns away. The man never appeared, though—just kept asking for money, and coming up with reasons why he couldn't return home. Finally, she had to accept that she'd been scammed. She stopped sending money and he disappeared. A report to the FBI went nowhere; she was told there was nothing they could do about it.

"I was just too in love to see it," she told us, after some years went by and she recovered from the heartbreak. She came away from the experience with four new rules for herself: to not let love blind her; to meet any potential partners in-person right away; to listen to her friends and family; and to never, never give anyone money.

In whatever way we meet a person of interest, checking out who they are is important for our safety. Scammers are indeed out there, and our best defense is to be good dating consumers and check for flaws before getting too involved.

 **GLORIA**

5. A pet will be safer.

It is amazing how many of my widowed, divorced, or single friends have gotten dogs. While I love dogs and have had many, I did not have a dog when my husband died, and I made the decision then not to get one. I didn't want the responsibility or the day-to-day chores. I was married at 21, and my marriage lasted for 60 years, so at the age of 81, I had finally discovered what it was like to not have a curfew or someone to be home for. I figured if I couldn't have my husband, I was going to enjoy the consolation of my freedom.

Furthermore, a divorced friend recommended that I say "yes" to any legitimate dating or outing opportunities for the next year, and I decided to follow her advice. Although it is nice to have a happy dog greet you at the door, it is also nice to be able to make a quick date decision or go to a movie or party on the spur of the moment. I don't have to worry about finding a dog sitter, and if I want to stay out late, I don't have to worry about what's happening to my rugs back home.

While it can be cozy to curl up with pets at night, I'd much rather have a human body in my bed. If you're of the same mindset, with a goal of finding love, then look for ways to simplify life in order to have the flexibility and time to search for "The One." If you currently have a dog, get a reliable dog sitter or a kennel, and embrace the opportunities that come along with dating.

 GLORIA

6. All the good people are already taken.
I can relate to this one! I thought that all the good guys were taken,

and after my first couple of attempts at dating, I didn't have reason to believe otherwise. True, I'd seen my grandchildren and their friends go on dating sites with a good amount of success. I don't mean that every date led to something meaningful or serious, necessarily, but they had fun and met some wonderful people. So, I approached it a bit more casually, and the next thing I knew, I'd met Frank and discovered a world that I didn't know existed for us seniors. Frank, who has more experience in this department, has met quite a few talented and beautiful women online, including a college professor, an artist, a speech therapist, a beauty salon owner, a nurse, and now me, a psychologist. Online dating is the real thing; there are people out there looking for love—millions of them.

7. I feel I'm being disloyal to my deceased partner or spouse.

We often hear widows and widowers say, "I had such a wonderful partner that I could never be with another person." Friends and family members who are also missing this departed partner often see this outlook as a badge of honor and courage, and so they encourage it. Obviously, though, these attitudes focus on the past, and can keep us stuck there. And the people who applaud singlehood don't have to grapple with loneliness.

What do *you* want your future to look like? If indeed you had a great partner, it means that you know how to be a great partner as well, and there is likely another satisfying relationship out there. It can be a difficult transition, but we've had great success with a couple of therapeutic interventions that we have used with clients who had these feelings of disloyalty. At the end of the chapter is an exercise we have found useful to deal with the feelings of being disloyal to a deceased partner and pursuing a new relationship. We sometimes need a way to resolve these feelings. The exercise helps to process our feelings and remind us that life is for living!

FRANK

8. It's easier to stick with paid sex or pornography.

This issue belongs overwhelmingly to men, who are far more likely to be drawn to sex workers or pornography as a substitute for dating. I've treated many men who found themselves in this category, and they had many experiences in common. For example, they'd stopped believing they could find someone whom they could trust and be close to emotionally. Several had stories about women being unfaithful or using them for their money. In such cases, their confidence had been badly shaken, and their primary goal was to protect themselves from experiencing that pain again.

To complicate the issue, our cultural norms say that men are supposed to be tough and not let things like this bother them. This is not the case, obviously, and it makes it more difficult for men to face or learn from a perceived failure. Many of us don't even have the ability to *admit* failure, let alone learn from it, so we will often retreat from real relationships to the artificial relationships we find in porn or paid sex workers.

Both of these experiences are based in the illusion of having control and seem to suggest a safe sort of intimacy: sex without the danger of pain. But they're strictly fantasy. The real pain for many is that they have lost confidence in their ability to have a real relationship of mutual safety, love, and respect.

One of my clients, Phillip, developed an addiction to porn after a couple of failures with women who had taken advantage of him. Both had expensive tastes and ran up credit card bills that he had a hard time paying off. Shaken by his bad luck, he turned to porn to protect himself. His addiction continued even after he found a new love and married. A few months into their marriage she discovered his addiction and told him she would leave him if he could not break himself of it. That's when he came to see me. In the course of therapy, he came to realize that he would turn to porn when he was upset, particularly when his anger revolved around his wife's spending. Once he discovered this connection, he was able to confront the issue of their different spending habits and develop better coping skills, which led him to break his addiction.

If you struggle with a pornography issue, I recommend finding a therapist who specializes in sexual addiction. It's very important to talk to someone. Cognitive therapy can also be very helpful in breaking and understanding habitual behaviors. In addition, look online for programs such as Sex Addicts Anonymous (SAA), which follows the same recovery model as Alcoholics Anonymous (AA).

9. Seniors like me will just get sick and die—
I don't want to be a caregiver!

Caregiving is a huge issue, especially for those of us who may have spent years as caregivers prior to losing a partner or spouse. This can happen to both men and women, but caregiving for a long-term partner prior to a death is much more likely to be "women's work." As we mentioned in the previous chapter, approximately 80 percent of women will be widowed. Long-term caregiving can lead to exhaustion and burnout, and the last thing many of us want when we return to dating is more of the same experience.

We were recently on a cruise ship from New York to England when we happened to sit down next to Nora, a well-groomed woman in her seventies. We quickly fell into conversation. Nora said that she was taking a ship to Europe rather than flying because she did not want to leave her dog, who had become her major companion after she'd lost her husband of 48 years to multiple sclerosis.

Over her husband's final ten years of life, her main activity had been caregiving. She had been widowed for seven years at that point and was traveling to see her family in Switzerland. When we told her how we'd met through an online dating site and that we were writing a book about dating, she became very animated, and asked all about the project and where she could get a copy of the book. It was clear that she loved the idea of finding love again, but she admitted that she didn't want another heavy round of caregiving responsibilities.

For women like Nora, being with a partner who does not have a premorbid condition is a major factor. A reminder, though: nobody is immortal, and there are no guarantees! You might be healthy and active right now, but if you have a partner through your last decades, you will probably be assisting one another with inevitable health issues. Assume, then, that some level of caregiving, at some point, is a given.

With this in mind, it's important to gather as much information as possible about a potential partner's health issues prior to moving into an advanced relationship. Clues in that partner's family history can provide insight. Still, have an open, honest conversation about your respective levels of health and feelings about caregiving and create a plan for the future. (We'll cover more about this in Chapter Seven.)

10. Why be open to criticism?

Criticism, especially from someone we care about, is painful, and too much criticism can destroy a relationship. But in the context of a long, close relationship, where partners are sharing your time and space, navigating health issues, and possibly juggling whole new sets of in-laws, some level of criticism is inevitable. We have great control over how we receive and respond to that criticism, however. One of the best professors I had at Columbia University once offered a re-frame of criticism that has stayed with me for my entire adult life. Most criticism from people we are close to, he said, is just "information about how they want you to show them love. It is only information."

If we think of criticism as information, then it can be helpful to show how to express love to a partner. Think of it as feedback from their perspective, from their personal experience. If we can keep from getting defensive and instead work to find the information about what our partner needs, then we'll be able to show love more effectively.

My professor, in his wisdom, went on to differentiate between "constructive criticism" and "shaming criticism." Constructive criticism is easier to hear as information. Shaming is an attack on someone's basic character. A statement like, "You left the dishes in the sink, and I wish you would clean them and put them away," is constructive: it's something that a partner can respond to, and it's not an attack on their fundamental character. "You are a jerk for leaving dishes in the sink," on the other hand, is shaming. It implies that the person left the dishes in the sink *because* he or she is a jerk, and so will always leave dishes in the sink.

Very few relationships can tolerate shaming criticism, which is often experienced as abusive, and rightfully so. However, if our partner offers constructive criticism, and if we can receive it as guidance rather than an attack, it can help make our relationship stronger. Our partner can feel loved when we respond to their need for change by doing things differently.

11. What if I don't find the right person the first time? Breaking up is difficult—I'll be stuck!

We refer to this as the fear of saying "no." To be successful in dating, consider the viewpoint of one of our clients, who said, "I know I will have to kiss a lot of frogs to find my prince." It's not likely to find a prince or princess on the very first date, so don't think about each suitor who doesn't turn into "The One" as a failure—instead, look at these dates as an inevitable part of the process. Make it a goal instead to have fun and learn a little more about what you want and don't want. If you can accomplish even one of those goals, then the date was a success. With this kind of thinking, we are more likely to spend less time with the wrong people.

Saying "no" to someone or having them say the same to us is difficult, but it's a very important life skill. If we can't say "no," then our "yes" doesn't mean anything. And it goes even deeper than that. Who we are comes from our ability to say "yes" or "no" to people and things in our life. We are all the products of our decisions about what we like and want and what we do not. Dating is one of the most important exercises we can conduct in forming this statement about who we are. If we have not developed the skill to be able to say "no" to someone, then we aren't ready for dating. Too many "yeses" can get a person into a lot of trouble!

If this skill is lacking, then find an assertiveness training class. The local community college's adult education department will likely have classes in assertiveness training. There are also a number of podcasts and online courses available. Therapy can also help.

It's essential to be able to say "no" (both in dating and in life!), so find a way to practice this skill. When we have confidence in this important area, then we can leave another fear behind.

Wrap-up

At this point in our lives, we've all been through an awful lot. Most of us have lost a partner through divorce or death. Yet we have survived, and in many ways, we have thrived and have learned about compassion and love. Many of us have experienced posttraumatic growth (more on this in Chapter Ten). Despite our setbacks, we've learned many lessons that will help us go forward and build the future we really want. Sometimes, all it takes is some understanding to bring clarity on the next steps.

After reading this chapter, if all you did was identify your concerns, you've already accomplished something important. Naming things takes away their power, just as turning on the light banishes a child's fear of what might be lurking nearby. Once you identify your concerns, you can figure out how to take your power back. Simply by thinking about what has been holding you back, you've already taken the first step in looking for "The One."

Now it's time to get excited. Remember, our goal here is to help start the process of experiencing all the dating the world has to offer. With that in mind, let's have some fun by exploring the best ways to find a potential partner.

Journal questions

- Ask which is greater: The pain of loneliness or the fear of what might happen if you date?
- Having read this chapter, write down as many things as possible that have held you back from entering the dating world.

Practice conversation

As we mentioned earlier in the chapter, if you are concerned that you are not honoring your lost partner by wanting a new relationship, we suggest the following: write a letter to your former partner, telling them how you are feeling without them and stating that you have a desire to find another relationship. Now reverse rolls and write a letter from them responding as you think they might. Continue the process until you feel some resolution. You might be surprised what comes up.

If you prefer conversation to writing, use the same back-and-forth process with a pair of chairs. Put the chairs face to face with a few feet in between. Then take one of the chairs and visualize your lost partner in the opposite chair. We have had clients who even added a picture of their loved one to make it more real. Then talk to the imagined person, expressing your desire to be in a new relationship. Next, move to the empty chair to provide a response from your absent partner (a response that, knowing them, they would make "from their higher self").

We have found both methods to be very helpful to clients when processing their feelings and reminding them that life is for living!

PART TWO

Senior
Dating

"NOT ON THE FIRST DATE."

CHAPTER THREE

Ready, Set, Go

In Part One, we did some heavy lifting, learning about the fundamentals of senior dating, facing relationship fears, and identifying desirable qualities in a partner. With the emotional and psychological groundwork complete, you are just about ready for senior dating. Before jumping in, though, there are a few practicalities to consider. Attention to these principles can make the dating experience easier and more enjoyable, an adventure rather than a series of tasks.

The central question, of course, is where to meet this special someone. We had a good friend who was excellent at fly fishing. When we asked him how he caught so many fish, he said, "Simple, I only fish in ponds where there are fish." The same applies to dating. If you want to meet single people, you must go where they are.

Our moms and dads met people at work, at church, at their universities, in bars or restaurants, and in dance halls and social clubs. They married their friends' friends or their sibling's friends or their neighbors—in other words, people they came across in everyday life.

Some of that still happens, of course, but today, most singles have taken their searches online, and now this is where a person can find the highest number of potential partners and have a chance to meet people with whom they would not normally come into contact. Estimates for the total number of users can vary, but there are easily tens of millions in the US, and hundreds of millions worldwide. According to the on-dating services, people over 50 are the fastest-growing segment of online singles. In fact, ABC's 2023 show *The Golden Bachelor* is highlighting the fact that the senior dating market is growing rapidly.

There are also a number of matchmaking services that take a more involved, customized approach in helping to find "The One." They involve higher fees, but instead of a computer algorithm that shows everybody in a geographic area, dating consumers work with a real live person who will screen potential suitors with the goal of offering a high level of compatibility from the get-go. If you're not looking forward to the adventure of lots of first dates, then a matchmaker can be a way to jump-start the process.

And then, of course, people still meet in the old-fashioned way, particularly if they're socially active and live in a place where regular patterns include contact with new people each week. In whatever way we're planning to meet someone, this chapter will help with finalizing those preparations and taking the first steps in the dating world. We'll focus our discussion on the online world since that's where things have probably changed most.

At this point, it's natural to feel a bit of trepidation. We want to emphasize that you'll have full control over those communications, and you can play it as safe as you need to in the beginning. Signing up for a dating app or a matchmaking service and creating a profile aren't a commitment to anything at all. Most apps even let you take those steps for free. At that point, you can browse the profiles of potential dates online from the comfort of the living room or while in your pajamas. There's no pressure. You'll have all the time you need to simply indulge the fantasy of looking at all of these possible future dates, while gaining the confidence that there just might be someone out there who could be interesting and fun. You can take the next step when you're good and ready.

Before all that, though, our first piece of advice is to line up support. Dating is a real adventure, and we don't have to go it alone!

Get a dating buddy

To help ensure the best dating experience, we highly recommend asking one or more friends or family members if they would join in on this dating adventure. Just knowing that there is someone there for you when striking out on this adventure can help keep things exciting and fun. A good dating buddy can also help keep hope alive and remind you that there is someone out there who is ready for love and companionship. If they have online dating experience themselves, they can also provide advice and wisdom as you find your way around and settle in.

If you are a little shy or get tongue-tied in one-on-one situations, a dating buddy can help you practice. We suggest asking the buddy to take the part of a prospective date and then to ask questions such as, "What are you looking for a partner?" and, "What do you like to do for fun?" Practice having a conversation with a buddy can help you to get warmed up for the real thing.

If you are extra anxious, use the following defensive technique that we have used with a number of clients with high anxiety. Pick the coffee shop to meet your first date. Go there with a dating buddy and sit at the table. Relax and have a cup of coffee or soft drink, then have the buddy ask the practice questions.

We have found these exercises to be not only fun but also enlightening; dating is a skill, and a bit of practice can go a long way. As with all matters of the heart, dating can contain some big ups and downs, and a buddy can also be there to laugh at the funny photos and stories and to hold your hand when you want to share those tender moments.

Our clients often tell us how much joy they find in sharing their experiences, thoughts, hopes, and dreams with their dating buddies. One of them, Jamie, called her dating buddy a "godsend." She was embarrassed to have what she called "teenage thoughts" while dating: would he call again? When would he kiss her? And why hadn't he called? "My married friends my age would see me as being silly or think I'd lost my mind," she said, "but my dating buddies listen with some wit and a sympathetic ear. Getting out those fears and concerns with my dating buddies has provided me with intense emotional relief."

Dating buddies can be young or old, but we have found grandchildren, friends younger than 25, and those older than 60 to be the most understanding, supportive, and willing to help. For practical advice or technical support, some of the best buddies can be found with the younger generations, for whom online dating is a completely natural part of life.

Lenora, a divorced mother of five, reported to us how much fun she had with her dating buddy, her twenty-five-year-old granddaughter. Her granddaughter is also dating, making her what we call a double dating buddy. They have fun filling out profiles and selecting photographs together and swiping through the pictures of potential candidates. Once a week they meet to check on each other's status. They share gales of laughter over profiles and advise each other on whom to reach out to. They have a friendly competition to see who can have the most coffee meetups in a month.

It can be helpful to have more than one buddy—we never know when we might have a quick meltdown, an exciting interaction, or a question, and want to be able to talk to someone on a moment's notice. If, like Lenora, you've got a grandchild as a dating buddy, you might also want to find someone closer to your age with whom to share adventures, particularly when they develop in areas you might not want to share with the grandkids! Put the word out that you are looking for support and your buddies will appear.

 # GLORIA

A little while after my husband Phil died, I was traveling with my granddaughter Eliza, who is in her late twenties. We were passing through southern Utah when I remembered I had a friend in the area, a geologist named Jerry who lives in Salt Lake City but often works in the field. I gave him a call and he happened to be in a nearby town. He came to join us, and he showed us around. He exhibited some interest in me, but I wasn't feeling the same way—he's younger than I am, and I hadn't started to think about such things anyway.

After watching all this, Eliza asked, "Grandma, don't you want to play the field?"

"Eliza," I said, sincerely, "there is no field at my age."

She laughed. "You might be surprised," she said.

Looking back, I think Eliza might have planted the seed. I knew that she had dated online and had met some interesting people and had some fun evenings. Eventually, of course, I'd take the plunge and sign up for a service, where I'd meet Frank.

After we got together, Frank and I had an opportunity to return the favor. We buddied up with our realtor, Sandra, and helped her to select an online site and to fill out her profile. When Frank and I relocated, leaving the hot Arizona summer for California, we continued to support her by phone. On our drive back to California, she called very excitedly to tell us that she had received 20 likes in the first week. We continue as her dating buddies and we enjoy hearing about her meet-ups. The last adventure was with a physician who cooked her an "amazing dinner." Frank and I have really enjoyed being her support buddies and have been overjoyed by her success.

Family support

While it may be easy to identify a friend to cheer you on, it can sometimes be a little more difficult to find support from others close to you. You may assume that they want the best for you but what they think is best may not be in sync with your hopes and dreams. It would be wise to ask these very important people how they feel about the decision to look for a life mate. It is not that they will make the decision on whether to look for a partner, but knowing where they stand can be an important factor in your pursuit. The only way to really know is to ask. Assumptions are not enough.

John, one of my clients, shared that he thought that he was ready to start the dating process after a messy divorce. I asked him what his friends and family thought about his decision. He said that he was sure that he would be supported by "all" of them. I suggested that he poll everybody to see if his assumptions were correct. He came back the next week and announced that he had been wrong. He had done as I asked and polled five male friends, his three siblings, and his mother. He said that they had appreciated being asked and gave him their most honest answers. His male friends thought it was great while two of his siblings and his mother thought he was jumping the gun. They were concerned it was too soon for him, and that he'd get into something he would later regret. This caused him to take a step back and reconsider where he was.

John's experience isn't uncommon. Change takes us into the unknown, and the unknown can give rise to fear. Even though this is your life, loved ones can have pretty strong feelings about how to navigate the periods following difficulties like death or divorce. So, when announcing the intention to find a partner, don't be surprised by their resistance.

It's also important to realize that we might be dealing with more than just individual opinions. In families especially, consider hierarchies. Some people have more influence than others, and family members can play different roles. In many cases, as with John's story, siblings may side with parents, who often hold a lot of power and sometimes even the purse strings.

If family support is important, it will save time and energy to go directly to the seat of power, rather than polling the whole family at the same time. John probably would have been better off talking directly to his mother. Addressing the powerful people first also honors their position. It can take some courage to have these conversations but remember: you're not a child anymore (far from it!), so you're not asking for permission. You're looking for support, which is different.

And as we'll repeat, only you can determine what's right for you, so use that knowledge to enter this process, take a stand, and explain to those around you what you're looking for and why the time is right. If it's important to have the support of friends and family, figure out who holds the power and set up a quiet meeting to share the reasons for wanting a relationship and your plans for finding "The One."

GLORIA

Beware the naysayers

A support system will be particularly valuable when dealing with those who might not be so enthusiastic about any new dating endeavors. Yes, we have noticed that when we mention online dating to many middle-aged people, the first thing they do is talk about the scams and dangers of meeting someone online. They'll often go on to talk about an article they read or an episode of *America's Most Wanted* about someone being exploited. While these incidents are not the norm, they can be a source of anxiety.

We recently had a personal experience talking with a lifestyle coordinator at a local senior community. We'd written a proposal stating that we were working to make dating safe and fun for people who had lost their mates and were living alone, and we approached her to ask if we could present to the members of the community. We thought we were providing a needed service, because we'd visited the community several times and we'd had conversations with residents who were excited by the topic. After we submitted our proposal, we heard nothing from the coordinator for two weeks. After several calls, we received the following response in an email:

> *Thank you so much, Mrs. Horsley.*
> *My team and I do not feel the subject matter*
> *of "Finding Love after Loss" and internet dat-*
> *ing are right for our community at this time.*

Neither of us give up very easily, so this just made us more determined to find out why our message was not "right" for the community. After several more calls, we were finally able to get an in-person meeting at her office. During the introductions, we could tell she was quite defensive. But I'm not one to beat around the bush, so I jumped right into the reason behind our visit.

"So why aren't we 'right' for this community?" I asked.

It turned out that the coordinator had participated in online dating and that she'd had some bad experiences. She went on to tell us that she thought that no one would attend our presentation. We countered that we were willing to take that chance and explained how we had talked to several of the residents, and they seemed interested in the subject matter. In the end, she relented but provided us with no support in the way of advertising our event.

As the lifestyle coordinator did, people might try to influence you about online dating when they have had their own negative experiences. However, keep in mind that these experiences likely come from the fact that online dating can be frustrating for those who have not done their homework and have not learned the rules of the road. So don't let one person's experience dictate your life. Don't let yourself be scared or intimidated by sensational news stories or negative comments.

We have a friend we'll call Joan who had been a widow for several years when her granddaughter told her how she'd met her own boyfriend on Tinder, a dating app, and suggested that Joan give it a try herself. Joan then called her son, Ned, on whom she had relied since his dad had died. She explained that she was lonely and wanted to try Tinder. Ned thought it would be a nice distraction and a lark for her and helped her set up a profile.

Things took a turn a few weeks later when Joan started communicating online with prospective men. She shared her excitement with Ned but also admitted she had fears about being scammed. She had also been cautioned by her priest that there were "men out there who were just waiting to take advantage of a good woman." Rather than supporting her in working through these concerns, he had a change of heart. "Mom," he said, "this just isn't for you." As a result, she discontinued her online membership and got a dog.

We learned about all this at Joan's funeral, where we encountered

Ned. We told him about our book on senior dating, which led him to open up and tell us his mom's dating story. He concluded with his regrets; he was sorry that he hadn't been more supportive of her finding a relationship. Although she'd enjoyed her dog, he told us, the last years of his mother's life were lonely.

Location, location, location

With support from dating buddies lined up and responses to the naysayers prepared, it's time to start thinking about how this all works on a practical level. One of the first questions to answer is how far to travel for a meet-up. In the opening section of this chapter, we talked about the millions of seniors dating online. Unless you've got a private jet, though, most of those millions of prospects are going to be pretty inconvenient to date. In a highly populated area such as Manhattan or Los Angeles, of course, there are lots of people of interest within a convenient radius. In a small town, there might only be a handful.

When signing up for a dating service, you'll be asked how many miles you are willing to go for a match. Think about your area, surroundings, and transportation options. On the outskirts of a big city, a large enough radius to take in the city's heart will mean many more choices. If in the country, then how far away are the neighboring towns? How many miles would you feel comfortable driving for a date? What if it's a dinner that might include a couple of drinks and a drive home through bad weather?

People tell us that with the opportunity to use video calls through a dating app, they are willing to specify longer distances in their search because they'll have a chance to have an initial conversation before deciding to travel a town or two away. Some people even like to include foreign possibilities as they want to meet people when they travel, or just like to meet up online with people from other countries.

One of our clients lives in Salt Lake City, Utah while her partner lives in Rochester, New York. They try to meet monthly in-person and they talk daily on the phone. They often plan the same meal and then cook and eat together while on a video call. As they approach retirement, they're looking forward to living together and spending lots of time skiing, one of their favorite shared activities.

When beginning this process, decide whether or not you are willing to have a long-distance relationship or prefer to find someone local. We prefer to be together, living in the same house, but others tell us that the old adage "absence makes the heart grow fonder" works for them.

Age is just a number.

Another question the service will ask, obviously, is about age. Maybe it doesn't seem like there should be much to discuss here, but the answer to this question can have some big implications.

If you have been lucky enough to have good health and to have aged well, then your stamina, appearance, and activity levels could well be typical of someone five or ten years younger. If so, then many suitors your age aren't going to be able to keep up. This problem afflicts women in particular, as many men tend to think that they should look for a younger woman, someone who is five or even ten years younger. (Remember the discussion back in Part One on men who date for status?) This strategy turns out to be a big disadvantage for women and a big mistake for men.

In order to maximize the pool of potential matches, we suggest you pause when considering your age. For some, perhaps due to ageist stereotypes or other beliefs about seniors' lifestyles, the age you *feel* could seem like a more accurate answer than chronological age. In that sense, listing an approximate age or an age range can also protect women from getting responses from prospects who are much older and/or less healthy. And with seniors, the level of health is a far more important indicator of compatibility than chronological age. There are people in their eighties—like Gloria—who are avid travelers and golfers, while others in their eighties have poor health that prevents them from scheduling much activity at all. The goal is to find that special someone out there, and if some creativity in this department increases your odds, we feel that's a big enough prize!

In our conversations with those who have dated online, we've discovered that fudging ages is a widespread practice. However, we also want to champion honesty in dating. So, while providing an approximate age ("a young 70-something" or "over 65") might be possible in an online dating app, we encourage disclosing your exact age early on once you strike up conversations. *A word of caution:* when it comes time to actually fill out a profile, be sure to review the service's policies. On some sites, users can't change their age without a lot of aggravation, including, in some cases, proof of age such as a driver's license or birth certificate.

In addition, if you decide to broaden the prospects in this way, we suggest going to friends, family, or dating buddies—anyone you can trust to be completely honest—to ask them for an "age assessment." Ask them how old you *seem*. Be careful, though. Their answer might not be what you hope, and this can be a bit of an ego blow. And if you choose to both provide an approximate age *and* ignore their assessment, it probably won't convince too many people.

 GLORIA

In my online profile, I did initially put down my exact age and was disappointed that almost all of the men who showed interest were five to ten years older. I am no spring chicken, but I've got a busy, active life and it was immediately clear that these guys were not able to keep up with me!

This is a real societal problem, as men continue to feel the need to search for younger women. This assumes that women will be equally drawn to older men, and while some of us are, things can shift quite a bit in our senior years, all of which creates a big asymmetry. As a result, we women find ourselves having to seek younger individuals just in order to find dating partners who match our activity levels. Frank, who is more understanding than most, was one of the only connections I made who wasn't significantly older than I am. In fact, I'm four years older than he is, and he makes for a wonderful companion since he's (usually!) able to match my energy levels.

Our friend Ruby was a professional dancer in Hollywood who had taken advantage of all the beauty enhancements available before she divorced at age 71. She decided to try an online dating site where she gave her true age. She found that the men who responded were mainly in their late seventies and early eighties. She met a couple of them but found that they didn't have her health or stamina. Ruby then moved to another senior site where she put her age as 65 (again, this would not be allowed on some dating sites) and luckily found that she had many more suitable matches. As soon as she developed rapport with someone, she'd tell them her real age. In her case, most of these men didn't care, and the ones who did weren't going to be a good fit for her anyway.

Ruby also had a cautionary tale, however, provided by her friend Marsha, who listed her own age as five years younger than she really was. Marsha met someone and they began dating, but she didn't reveal her true age. After several months she still hadn't told him, and her anxiety about it continued to rise. So, if you decide to take this route, *make a conscious decision about when you will reveal your precise age.*

Get familiar with the different services.

There are upwards of 8,000 dating services around the world these days and growing! Does this mean there's a massive research project in front of you? No, it does not. Consider that many of these will be overseas or in foreign languages, so unless you're open to finding someone in Lithuania, you don't need to think about the majority of those services. In the US, there are a handful of established, general-interest sites where most of the action can be found these days. Of those, lots of articles and reviews are also available from people who have already done the work of checking them out and compiling their findings. Some great resources might be available in the experiences and recommendations of your dating buddies and other supporters. This is where your kids or grandkids might have valuable opinions and insights.

We met on Silver Singles, a site for those of us fifty and up, which offers both hetero and same-sex dating options. OurTime is another such service. Other popular sites, which are not specifically geared for seniors but where many of us can be found, include:

- Bumble
- Hinge
- Match
- OKCupid
- Plenty of Fish
- Tinder
- Zoosk

While the goals of these services are the same, they take a variety of approaches and features, with new innovations coming out all the time. Zoosk, for example, offers online touring adventures, such as a virtual date online and exploring cities such as Paris, Kyoto, or New Orleans together. Other sites cater to specific interests and preferences, whether in regard to religion, ethnicity, political leanings, or sexual preference. We've seen our clients find success on sites like the following:

- BlackPeopleMeet
- Catholic Singles
- Grindr (for gay men)
- Her (for gay women)
- Jdate (for Jewish singles)
- Mormon Match
- Stir (for single parents)

With the speed of change online, a print guide to these services would quickly be outdated, so our best advice is to get on the internet and do a bit of research about the best sites for your age and interests. You may eventually decide to join a few different sites, but we would suggest that settling on a single one to start, so you don't get overwhelmed. Remember our realtor friend, who got attention from 20 different men in her first week on the site? That one site gave her more than enough to explore for her introduction to online dating. This should be a lighthearted adventure, not an overwhelming burden!

Matchmaking services

Online services will show profiles for everyone in your age range and geographical area, but matchmaking services aim to provide results based on quality rather than quantity. Our friend Sandra, for whom we're dating buddies, decided to try out one such service, in conjunction with her online subscriptions. She was given an option of three matches for $2,500 or $5,000 for six matches and decided to go with the deluxe package. The process began with a video interview when the matchmaker, Gwen, asked Sandra all about herself.

She was a little surprised to discover that the profiles of her eventual matches would come to her without photographs. When she asked why, Gwen explained that all the men she'd be introduced to would be pre-screened, and that the human tendency to dismiss people quickly based on a moment's assessment of appearance would work against her. The service had better results when both people showed up without biases about appearance, ready to sit and talk and get to know each other.

A few days after the intake interview, Gwen reached out to Sandra with her first match and a reservation at a high-end restaurant. She received a profile that not only lacked a photograph, but also the man's name—she received that two hours before the date was to start. That date wasn't a winner—the guy frequently brought up women's body types. The second date wasn't much better; he was someone she'd actually met on Silver Singles who had blown her off previously. When she asked Gwen where they found their matches, she was told that was proprietary information, which led Sandra to suspect that they, too, were trawling the online services, looking for participants who might be a good match for their service. The service was looking to catch fish where the fish were.

When considering a matchmaking service, make a few a calls and then get some quotes. Understand that they don't have a secret stash of singles tucked away; they are pulling from the same pool of potential dates who are already out there, looking for their own matches. The matchmaking services provide value through customized screening and vetting, so make the decision based on how valuable those are to you.

When we last caught up with Sandra, she was having fun dating people she'd met in a variety of ways. Her two further matchmaking dates hadn't led her to "The One," but one of them had been with the owner of an Arabian horse farm, and she'd re-discovered her love of riding. She was looking forward to her remaining two matches, exploring a new friendship with someone she'd met through a mutual friend, and keeping an eye on her Silver Singles account. All this, after she'd told us, "I thought it was all over for me after I turned 70!"

Wrap-up

Whether signing up for a matchmaking service or a dating app, the key point is to put out the intention and tell the unconscious mind that you are ready to date. That message causes the brain to act and behave differently, especially once you verbalize those intentions to friends and family. When sending out the message, "Hey, I am ready for a relationship," you will naturally be more interested in people as potential dates, looking for things that you have in common, and being more accepting of a warm handshake, hug, or a hand on the shoulder. You may even find friends and family on the lookout. It can all start with that first small intention.

In this chapter, we wanted to address a few of the big questions we've fielded from our clients and heard from our friends and family as they prepared to embark on their own senior dating adventures. Many of you are stepping into some pretty unfamiliar waters here, though, and are likely to have several more questions. We can relate. Gloria, if you recall, had been married for more than 60 years—she hadn't dated since Eisenhower was in the White House. When she decided to test-drive online dating, she had a whole list of what-ifs, and you probably do too.

But as with any human endeavor, it's impossible to anticipate and prepare for every eventuality. We can't learn how to swim in a classroom; at some point, we've just got to jump into the pool. In the next chapter, we'll offer guidance on those first few steps, taking care to answer as many questions as possible, and to address as many facets of dating and romance as we can. So, get that swimsuit on—it's time to test the waters!

Journal questions

- What kind of family support will you have as you start on this journey?
- How far are you willing to travel to date?
- How old do you feel? How will you reflect that age in your dating profile?
- Which online dating site(s) are you drawn to?

Practice conversation

How will you talk to family and friends about a relationship? Visualize telling loved ones about your significant other and write down what you'll say.

"I HAVE AN ONLINE DATING ADVISOR."

CHAPTER FOUR

Online Dating: A User's Guide

With the groundwork and the preliminary considerations complete, it's time to take the plunge! Take a casual approach. Think of it as a party you've been invited to, and you're simply going to pop in and see what's happening. With an easy approach in mind, then, it's time to put on party clothes! Here are the first steps:

1. Choose a dating service
2. Fill out a profile
3. Browse the other profiles and consider expressing interest
4. Make contact
5. Check it out and be safe
6. Connect in person
7. Follow up after the first date
8. Learn from early experiences and keep at it!

Choose a dating service

Based on the preliminary explorations in the last chapter, does one particular site rise to the top? If so, then go ahead and create an account. If not, spend a little more time researching, but don't over-think it! Plug "senior dating sites" into the internet browser's search bar and from the results, explore whichever one resonates.

Many sites will let users set up a profile for free but have a credit card handy pretty early in the process, as you won't get too far without it. These services are complex and expensive to operate, and membership fees keep the companies going. Usually, you'll be offered different options for how long you want to stay signed up. You can always extend the time so there's no need to commit to a long time in the beginning. Consider signing up for a month—you'll learn a lot about the service in that time and can use that information to make the next decision.

Beyond the basic subscriptions, many services offer upgrades and options to entice users to spend more money. Until you are comfortable with the site, we suggest staying with the basics. If you're drawn to some of the premium features, though, and the upgrades aren't a problem for your budget, then go for it.

Many people end up on a number of sites, with slight variations of the same profile, but we recommend starting with just one. After learning the basics, you'll be in a better position to judge whether or not an alternate service might offer something different or complementary. At that point, if you're looking for more action, you can change sites or add more. In the beginning, though, one will offer plenty to learn from and do.

 # GLORIA

When I started my own online dating adventure, I didn't know anything about it at all. In fact, I wasn't even looking for someone. You might recall that I had just ended what Frank and I call an "almost experience." I was stuck in a hotel room in Hawaii with COVID, trying to get my head around some feelings of hurt and anger. What better way to process my feelings, I figured, than to write a book? I'd include a chapter on online dating, which meant that I had to learn a little something about it.

I started by searching for sites for people over sixty and came up with Silver Singles. I signed up, paid the fees, and started to explore the site. For my profile, I gave my exact age and used my middle name, Jeannie. Putting my middle name made me feel safe but also true to myself. I was on my way. The interest came pretty quickly. Most of the guys who reached out, as I mentioned, were several years older than I was, but it was still fun to see the possibilities. I had only a few connections when I got lucky and found Frank.

Not every story goes quite so well, so early, but connections like these *do* happen every day. Based on my own experience, the stories from my clients, and the events I've witnessed with my own children and grandchildren, I am today one of the biggest cheerleaders for online dating. I wish you all the luck and the great success that Frank and I have had.

Fill out a profile

Once you've selected a service and set up your account, it's time to complete a profile. As you'll see, there are as many different ways to do this as there are singles online. Some people write their autobiographies, others only share a few words. Some people go for a casual, humorous tone, while others take a more serious or romantic approach. We have seen that many singles—especially those of the younger generations—take steps to portray themselves as glamorous and adventurous. Their goal is to advertise themselves, so they'll stand out from the others.

At this point in our lives, though, we don't need to sell ourselves, so we suggest a different approach. Rather than trying to impress, use your profile to state what you want and need in a partner. "Looking for someone, not Mister Perfect, but must be genuine, honest, kind, friendly, sensitive, a good listener (in other words, a Boy Scout). Must be fiscally responsible and interested in a long-term relationship." Try to keep it brief while conveying a sense of humor and compassion. Let the world know what you want and, as with any job, "only those qualified need apply."

Remember all that work we did in Chapter One to figure out what's important in a relationship? We talked about compatibility in the realms of religion, politics, finances, activity level, travel, family needs, and so on. Use the material developed earlier about your heart's desires to tell the world what type of partner you are looking for. Select a few of the most important aspects and feature them in your profile. Weave these together with details about yourself as you go.

For example, if you've got a big family and you're looking for someone who will be able to fit into your family trips or gatherings, you might write, "I'm looking for a partner who will stay up late and beat my ten grandkids at gin rummy." If you're looking for a travel companion, be specific: "I'm looking for someone to explore Italy with me next year." This reveals a bit about who you are, but more importantly, it tells others what you need.

The profile is important, so don't rush through it. Give it some time and thought. Share a draft of the profile with a dating buddy for another perspective and be open to their feedback.

The description is just one part of your profile, of course. The other part—the part everyone will see first—is the photograph. We suggest a simple, current photograph, without anyone else in it. Consider having pictures that are related to your description. If you like to travel, include a travel photo. If you like tennis or pickleball, or if you like to dance, use those photos. You'll likely have a chance to post a few different images; by selecting one of them as the primary image, it will be the first thing people see when the profile pops up.

It can be pretty tempting to include a photo that looks maximally spectacular. Maybe that shot from the holiday party ten years ago captures something about you that you really want others to see, or maybe you're planning to lose ten pounds, so you decide to post a photo from before having put on those pounds on in the first place. And there are all those photo filters, which can transform a photo with the push of a button.

Take it from us, though: resist this temptation! It's a terrible waste of time to not present a real picture of who you are, right now, today. While those old or edited photos might increase the amount of initial interest, what happens next? Think about the long-term plan. You're looking for somebody who will embrace you for exactly who you are, so why start out with a photo that *isn't* exactly who you are?

Of course, appearance isn't everything. It would be great if there could be less of an emphasis on looks, but we aren't going to be able to change everyone's mind anytime soon. We'd like to encourage you, however, not to place too much emphasis on those photographs. In-person chemistry is much more important, so try to be open to those first date offers, even if the image doesn't quite match what you have in your head. Remember the discussion of matchmaking services in the previous chapter? They withhold those photos intentionally because of our tendency to place way too much emphasis on appearance.

That said, it can be very disconcerting to meet someone who doesn't look anything like their photo. (We always find it strange and rather amusing when we come across an obituary for someone who died in their nineties but that features a photo of someone in their fifties.) Gloria sits on a board with a friend who is in her sixties who uses a college photograph of herself. Time to update that photo, we'd say! We've had clients tell us that as many as 40 percent of the people that they met for in-person dates did not look like the photos on their profile. We see this not as a problem that relates to appearance, or surface-level notions of beauty, but as a question of building trust. If a suitor cannot represent themselves honestly in something as simple as a profile photograph, then what does that say about their tendencies to misrepresent or hide things, or to outright lie?

Frank once connected with a woman, and after texting for a bit, they decided to get together for an in-person evening. When he arrived, though, he found that she was 20 pounds heavier than she had been in her picture. Frank has nothing against the heavier among us, so the extra weight itself wasn't a disqualifier. She'd misrepresented herself, though, and with that initial breach of trust, there was no chance of a second date.

Besides appearance, consider what else the photograph is saying and make sure you're representing your concerns, activities, and economic status accurately. That Maserati in the dealership showroom as a background could lead to a lot of uncomfortable explanations when you show up to those first dates in a Ford. Overselling yourself in the profile will mean negative surprises on first dates, and those will quickly lead to rejections, which, in turn, can take a major toll on your self-image. You deserve to be loved and wanted for who you are, so start there. It's well worth it to trade that initial attention for a greater chance at somebody who will stand by you in the long term. Someone out there is looking for the real you!

Finally, be careful about including photos with other people in them. It's not uncommon for some people to post photos with groups of friends, which can sometimes lead to suitors being confused about which face is yours. One of my clients included a photo with her son, and prospective dates thought that it meant she was interested in dating far younger men. If you're still struggling to decide on a set of images, share a few options with your friends or dating buddies and ask them which ones present you honestly and in the best light.

When struggling with the technology, seek out help. There are many sites out there, and some are easier than others to use. If you get stuck, try not to get discouraged. Take a break and ask someone for help. Many clients find helpful resources in their children or grandchildren, and others find guidance through the service's own customer support representatives, who can often be reached via telephone.

And for goodness' sake, take the time to figure out the software, so that all photos are cropped correctly, aligned, and right-side-up. One of our clients, a banker, posted a sideways picture. It didn't work out too well for him. Even if struggling initially with the profile, don't rush through this step. It's important to be able to navigate their tools and features and to put together an accurate profile, so take your time. After the profile is set up, things will move along, and you can enjoy meeting new people.

Browse the other profiles and consider expressing interest
Now comes the fun part: seeing what's out there! There's no right or wrong way to do this. Spend as much or as little time flipping through the other profiles as you like. If someone interests you, the service will offer some way—or several ways!—of signaling that interest. At the same time, you'll begin to receive notifications of others who are interested in you. Most services have a way of indicating a new profile, which can translate into a lot of initial interest.

Remember how Sandra got notifications from 20 different men right after her profile went live? That might not be a typical debut, but it can happen!

When starting to receive these notifications, we suggest splitting them into three categories: interested, not interested, and almost of interest. If "not interested," simply ignore them. The service will give some way to clear them out. At this initial stage, these are very casual connections, with very little time invested in them, so don't worry about letting someone down.

Depending on the service, you might also receive a personal note from someone you don't want to connect with. While this can be awkward, it's a regular occurrence in online dating, and something to get used to; don't waste energy feeling like you're disappointing someone. Don't pressure yourself to reply or jump into conversations you don't want to have.

For those who are a "maybe," simply leave them where they are. There's no hurry to decide. With more experience, you might decide to reach out with a "like" or a personal note to see if they're still available and interested.

And when choosing to respond, remember to be gentle with yourself and others. As always, treat others the way you would want to be treated if someone doesn't reciprocate your interest. We are all vulnerable, so let's each do our part to make these services safe.

Of course, the real excitement starts when users exchange mutual interest and decide to reach out. First, decide on the communication style that is most comfortable for you, such as texting. Some of the services include phone calls or video calls right in the app, so that there's no need to send your contact information if you don't want to. Reach out and see where the conversation goes!

It's easy enough when the process is straightforward, but at this point there are a couple of small things to prepare for. First, don't be surprised by quick changes of heart. Someone might express interest one day but then ignore messages the next. Try not to take it too personally. It probably just means that someone else popped up in the meantime and got their attention, and this might well happen at some point. We all have limited time and attention.

Also, it can be quite common to have a number of conversations develop at once, and in cases like this, some people have some difficulty deciding where to put their energy. If so, we suggest taking it slowly so you can keep enjoying the process. Try not to let it cause stress.

In the online dating world, it's actually quite common to schedule first dates with a number of different people. If that's your style, then go for it! You'll know when it's time to focus. If not, then just take it slowly and allow a front-runner to emerge.

Check them out and be safe

While the majority of people on the sites are honest, well-intentioned singles, there are a handful of bad apples in the bunch, so we suggest a few easy steps to take early on to protect yourself, your time, and your energy. Most dating services don't provide any verification that people are who they say they are, so it's incumbent on you to do a bit of legwork. We call this being a "good consumer."

Know what the realities are and know how to deal with them, and then relax and enjoy yourself.

We've mentioned, and will discuss further, those people who misrepresent themselves, whether with outdated photos or inaccurate descriptions. Those people just come with the territory, unfortunately, and there's no foolproof way to avoid them entirely. Those aren't the bad apples we're talking about here, though. There are a small number of out-and-out scammers who sneak into these services and set up totally fake profiles.

There's nothing unique about this in the online world; scamming has been around for centuries. Gloria's uncle, Mark, once bought what he thought was a bag of wheat, only to find out it was birdseed. Many an unsuspecting widow has been sold an unnecessary new roof for her house. In the online world, though, the difference is that scammers can be connected to millions of potential targets around the world without leaving their living rooms. It's a problem that isn't going away. It can happen to both women and men, so the best defense is to equip yourself to figure out their tricks early. This will help to make you a good consumer and keep you safe.

First and foremost, if anyone asks for money or private information, cut off the conversation *immediately*. If you think this person is not on the up-and-up, report them. This is also part of being a good consumer: doing your part to help the services keep their sites free of scammers.

FRANK

Jim, a client of mine, was skeptical of going online even though he was lonely and had not had a relationship in years. With my encouragement, he decided to sign up for a dating site exclusively for singles aged 50 and up. He was surprised and excited when he got some interest right away. The interested woman was, however, out of state, and he had to communicate by texts and email. I had cautioned him, as I do with all my clients, that he should conduct an internet search on her and perhaps use a more involved service to search public records. Jim took my advice and came back and told me that he had discovered she was not who she seemed. She had been married several times and had a DUI on her record. He contacted the dating service and told them about her profile.

Connect in person

If a conversation is going well, and you're confident that the person is who they say they are, the next step is to meet in person. This is probably the most pivotal moment in the online dating process since you'll quickly discover whether or not it's a connection worth pursuing. The time it takes to progress to this stage can vary quite a bit from one person to the next, but our recommendation is to have this first in-person meet-up sooner rather than later. We've heard too many stories from clients about how they'd developed strong feelings and attachments through intimate text exchanges, only to later discover that the person they're talking to isn't who they pretended to be. If this turns out to be the case, put on your big-girl or big-boy pants, as the saying goes, and figure out how to discontinue things graciously.

Unfortunately, not everyone will represent themselves in a forthright way. Our friend Jill, who has been active in online dating for some time, calls these people "pretenders." She spends as little time as possible with texting or phone calls, and instead likes to get right to an in-person meeting. You won't know who you're dealing with until that in-person opportunity, so as soon as it feels comfortable, decide on a safe way to meet.

Where and when should one do this? For that first in-person meeting, we suggest an afternoon cup of coffee or tea at a café. Keep it brief—about an hour or so will give plenty of information to decide if you want to see them again, perhaps progressing to dinner and drinks or more elaborate outings. If there isn't a connection, an hour at a coffee shop goes by faster and more painlessly than a meal out.

Jill has developed a very no-nonsense approach to those first coffee dates. She has one of her dating buddies call her 15 minutes after the date starts. If she's enjoying herself, she won't answer the telephone. If she isn't, she answers the phone and then excuses herself, saying she has an emergency at home. Some might find her way of leaving a meet-up harsh, but she believes that it is kinder to make a quick exit once she knows the relationship isn't for her.

We are not suggesting doing it her way; everyone has to decide for themselves how they can gently turn someone down. Jill developed her system because she is a busy woman who knows exactly what she's looking for. There are many other approaches, though. Whatever your capacity is for less-than-stellar first dates, you'll save aggravation and disappointment by managing expectations carefully. Try to remain curious and meet your date like a new friend in the sandbox. Share your shovel and bucket and greet them as a playmate rather than a possible partner for life. This will take a lot of the pressure off and keep you open to having a good time or making an interesting new connection.

FRANK

Although I was a veteran of online dating when we met, Gloria was brand-new at it, and she broke several of the unwritten rules right out of the gate. It just happened to work out beautifully for us, but when we tell the story, we have a good laugh about it, given all that we've learned and discussed since. I've got her permission to share it here, so our example can illustrate how to start playing the online dating game.

When I saw Gloria's profile—a.k.a. "Jeannie"—on the dating app, I was intrigued. Here was an attractive woman who was running a foundation with her daughters. She was a psychologist, like me, and had been a nurse before getting her PhD. A golfer, she was in great shape, and she liked classic movies. In her pictures she had the most loving smile. She just stood out from the other profiles. It did not take me long to decide to send a "like" to her online. I asked if she would check out my profile and see if she might be interested in meeting me.

She responded with a text saying that indeed she would be interested in meeting, and she told me she was out of town at that time but would be back on the following Monday. As we were making plans for that meeting, she went off-script for the first time. I suggested that we meet for afternoon coffee, as this was what I had learned to do when setting up the first in-person contact. Compared to an evening meal or a date with drinks, it's safer and there's less pressure, and as we all know, alcohol tends to cloud good judgment.

Gloria, however, said that she wanted to meet for happy hour at a local restaurant. I was surprised and impressed by what I took as a sign of her confidence. Almost all of the first dates I'd been on previously had gone for the innocuous coffee option, and her suggestion of an evening with drinks intrigued me greatly. We continued to text while she was out of town, trading information about professional backgrounds and our work in our respective communities, and when she returned to town, we met at a casual but upscale restaurant in Scottsdale.

We settled into our night and struck up a wonderful conversation about our common experiences as therapists, about her foundation, which focuses on supporting people through the process of grief, and about my interest in sculpting. I had been sculpting for many years and had turned my home into a studio and gallery with more than 50 different sculptures displayed. We were just finishing dinner when I decided to toss in a little humor.

"Why don't you come up to see my etchings?" I asked her, with a chuckle. If you're younger than we are, you might not get the joke: it's a thinly veiled pick-up line that dates all the way back to the thirties and forties, used by men to lure dates into their bedrooms. I knew she'd get it, and with the way our conversation was going I figured I'd get a laugh. This is when she broke the next rule, which left me twice as stunned as the first.

"Yes, I'd love to," she said, and then casually took another sip of her cocktail.

I barely recovered. "Now?" I asked.

"Yes," she said. And then she immediately jumped right into another big no-no! "I was wondering if you could give me a ride home?" she asked. "My car is in the repair shop and my friend who brought me here is not going to be able to pick me up after all."

Never before in my dating experience had I met someone with the confidence and assertiveness to state exactly what she wanted and not to think twice. We left the restaurant, and after a stop at my place to take a look at my sculptures—yes, to literally look at my sculptures!—I took her back to her place. We soon set up a time for a second meeting and now we are together and enjoying our senior dating experience.

Gloria would be the first to tell you *not* to follow her example. I'm a perfect gentleman, of course, so it worked out well for us, but some might have had other motives, and would have sought to take advantage of Gloria's fearlessness. Until you're more familiar with someone, we'd advise you to meet in public where it's easier to make an exit if you don't like how things are feeling, and also to have your own transportation ready to go. Play it cautiously in the beginning, and then relax into things as you get to know each other better and comfort develops.

While it's always prudent to start out a little bit guarded, that's only because of the relatively few bad apples in the bunch. Most people don't have ill intentions, and we hear from our clients about all sorts of enjoyable connections and adventures, even when they come across someone who doesn't seem to be destined to be a life partner. Millions of others *do* end up finding that special someone, though, once they take the chance.

So, what if the first date seems to be going in that direction? Let's say you're well into that first meet-up and everything is going nicely, and you'd like to see this person again. In this case, we think it's important to clearly indicate this, right there in the moment. It can be difficult for some—particularly women, because of social conditioning—to be this assertive, but there are easy ways to bring it up. For example, test the waters by exploring mutual interests. If both people are interested in sports, theater, or music, for example, ask them if they would like to participate in one of these activities. The level of enthusiasm in their response will indicate pretty quickly whether they are interested in a second date or not.

It can also happen that some people will agree to a second date at the moment, but do not actually intend to keep it. Some people see this as a way of avoiding an awkward interchange, while others might see it as a gentler way of addressing someone else's feelings. We encourage senior dating partners *not* to do this; it's misleading and manipulative. If someone is not interested in a second meeting, they have a right to their feelings. So, be honest and direct. It's respectful, even if it isn't what a date might want to hear.

Follow up after the first date

In all likelihood, most first meetings won't lead to a second date. When we tally up all the stories we've heard and add our own personal experiences, we arrive at a fairly common number: about 60 percent of the people met online will not have represented themselves accurately. This is a shame and a colossal waste of time, and we hope the culture and practices around this will change. As these people find that their misrepresentation is disappointing more and more of their dates, maybe there will be a shift. But for now, though, this is just how it is.

We have also found that of the other 40 percent, many will have qualities, attitudes, or interests that will keep them from being good candidates. But remember, when looking for the one, it's the most important role someone can play in your life, and vice versa. With something this important, take time to get it right.

For whatever reason, if you're not interested in pursuing someone, we encourage kindness. Even if they misrepresented themselves and then turn out to be a terrible conversationalist, or even if they're on the opposite side of some important beliefs, remember that they're going through many of the same things in terms of their search and all the vulnerability it entails. They are responsible for managing their feelings. Treat everyone with respect and dignity, and you'll be able to navigate those subpar first dates with grace.

It can also happen, of course, that one person had a good time and developed the beginnings of an attraction, only to find out the other person didn't feel the same way. You could be on the receiving end of a rejection that might or might not be as respectful as one would hope. This can be a fragile moment for the ego. If this happens, just remember that we're looking for someone who is as taken with us as we are with them at that first meeting. There will be times when those don't align, but again, you're looking for that special person.

FRANK

A number of clients involved in online dating ask what to do if they're not interested in a second date. One way is to express appreciation for the meeting while stating that this is not what you are looking for. There's no need to go into details unless asked, and even then, it's your prerogative how much you care to share. Most people will not ask, I've found. I like to be honest, so I don't waste their time. Secondly, I wish them luck in finding someone who is right for them. I have found that the direct and honest method usually works best.

Over my online dating life, which now spans several years, I have found that out of every 20 women I met, only one or two were people of interest, with whom I thought I might develop a lasting relationship. That being said, it was well worth the effort, as I have also had some excellent meet-ups and connected with some really interesting and talented women.

Learn from early experiences and keep at it!

In the beginning, it can feel like a big investment of time and energy to get a profile set up just right, start those conversations, verify you're talking to real people, and get to the point when meeting those people. Again, think of it as a fun adventure, a way to connect with and learn about other people. Keep that job interview metaphor in mind. When hiring for a job, if there are a hundred different applicants, we don't go in expecting the very first candidate to be the best qualified. Instead, we devote some time to the process and conduct a thorough search, knowing that the extra care and deliberation will pay off in the end. Love and companionship are a much bigger prize than a job, so approach the search with even more care and patience.

We recently had a chance to catch up at a party with Stacey, an old friend of Gloria's. Stacey is a successful insurance broker who owns a business in Los Angeles. When her husband Brian passed away many years ago, she felt lonely and decided to try online dating. She said that she was very scared, but her loneliness propelled her. She was excited when she received a message from a man whose profile she liked, and whom she thought would be a great match. He was also an insurance broker who owned his own business. He was in his seventies and had a professional-looking picture. She talked to him on the telephone several times and was excited about the prospects of this new relationship.

They scheduled their first meet-up at a popular coffee shop. Stacey's sister and niece went with her for support and sat in the corner of the shop. Stacey recounted that when the guy appeared he was nothing like the conservative man in his picture. He was wearing jeans, a black muscle shirt, chains around his neck, and he had a big chain linking his wallet with his back pocket. Stacey said that she felt scared and frustrated. There was a bit of comic relief in that she could see her sister and niece laughing in the corner of the shop, but overall, it was a miserable, discouraging experience. She felt she had failed, and she removed her profile and never went back.

Ten years later, as she reflected, she said that she wished she had continued to date online. She had started a "platonic relationship" with an old friend whose wife had died, but when she saw us together it reminded her of what she was missing. She told us that she regretted giving up because she missed being with a man who excites her desire and passion.

Wrap-up

We firmly believe there's someone out there for you. Don't give up and settle for less. You're not going to find the love of your life by hiding in the house, so keep going forward. Keep interviewing those candidates! Expect a mix of good and challenging experiences, perhaps an "almost experience" or two. Just think of them all as learning experiences, as preparation for finding the one that makes your heart sing.

If you have found a person of interest and have moved on to a second date or beyond, you might begin to encounter intimacy issues. Perhaps it's time to look at what you want and desire in the area of sexuality. Now is the time to take a thoughtful approach to getting your needs and wants met. In the next chapter we discuss the often-neglected area of senior sex. Our friend Gary, a nuclear scientist, used to tell his boys that there are two brains: the big brain and the small brain, and when involved with girls they should use the big brain before the small. In love as in life, let your big brain be your guide.

Journal questions

- Write a sentence describing you and your interests to use in a dating profile.
- After matching with someone online, verifying their identity, and getting to know each other online, think about a good place to meet in person.

Practice conversation

How will you initiate a conversation with someone of interest? Take a second to write out a message to send someone online to make that first connection. Start by saying hello! And introduce yourself.

"WOULD YOU LIKE TO COME IN AND HELP ME EXTEND MY LIFESPAN?"

CHAPTER FIVE

Through the Bedroom Door

Let's say you've met someone. That first coffee meet-up was full of scintillating conversation and laughter, and then there was a lunch date that made you want to cancel your afternoon plans. Now you're at dinner, locked in prolonged eye contact before the entrees have even arrived. It's exhilarating, but in the back of your mind you can't help but think about how long it's been since you last navigated through new love...

You might be wondering if your body will work the same way it did then, perhaps thinking: where will we go? Their place? My place? If it is my place, do I keep the pictures of my former partner around? When do I take off my wedding ring? What if the kids drop in? Should I tell them I am going out of town? What will the neighbors think? Should I ask my date to park the car down the block? Should they stay overnight, or should I send them home? Should I buy some new underwear or lingerie or just make it look sponta-neous and wear the old stuff? What if they snore? What if *I* snore? Will they be uncomfortable with my medical regimen? What will they think about the fact that I wear hearing aids? And what will they think of my body? What if I can't perform or have an orgasm?

For many of us, going to bed with a new partner after a hiatus of months or possibly years is a big step. And while it might have been pretty instinctive when we were younger, at this age there are a lot of new things to think about when considering sharing someone's bed for the first time. We have found that many of our clients come in needing to process various aspects of that first sexual experience, aspects that can sometimes be quite unexpected and surprising.

In this very direct chapter about sex, we'll go through the most common questions we get asked about sexual intimacy in the world of mature dating. Much has changed since our younger years, and some of it, frankly, for the worse. For example, our bodies don't look or work quite the same, which can present some challenges we didn't have to face before.

But another set of things have changed for the better. We know ourselves and what we want, and we're able to communicate with more ease and confidence. We're wiser and more patient, and when we learn how to make those assets a part of intimacy, they can bring their own pleasures. With a bit of foreknowledge, you can make it through dessert and whatever might come after with the same fear-lessness you used to get this far.

Senior bodies

When most of us think about how sex is different in later years, we think first of our changing bodies. It's clear why this would be the tendency: our bodies are right there in front of us, in the mirror every day. We might see the growing lumps and bumps. Many women have told us that they feel embarrassed about their older bodies, breasts, and bellies. Men have expressed their concerns about their waistlines and jawlines and losing hair or going gray. Turning the lights down low and disappearing under the covers can address some signs of aging, of course, but another set of changes also comes into play.

FRANK

Due to age and health issues, the days of a full erection may be over for many men, especially those over 70. According to the Cleveland Clinic, 70 percent of men in this age group are affected by erectile dysfunction (ED). I've counseled many men over the years about their issues with ED, resulting in a number of different outcomes, including many good ones. There are ways to navigate this with grace and ease if you know how. Otherwise, this condition can lead to embarrassment and can even tank a promising relationship.

One of the first things to do is to *talk with your doctor*. There are a number of simple factors that can contribute to ED, such as medications or smoking, which impacts the fine blood vessels in the penis. Be aware that different doctors can approach this in very different ways, though.

Gloria had a client once named Pamela who had been widowed for a year when she made an appointment to discuss a frustrating sexual experience with Leonard, a new partner. During her first night with her new beau, she discovered that Leonard could not get an erection strong enough to have intercourse. Afterwards, he made an appointment with his urologist, who gave him pamphlets advertising penile pumps, a technique for putting a constrictive ring around the penis, and some prescriptions. He showed up for their next night together with a bag of syringes and asked her if she would give him a shot.

Pamela, who was a nurse, was appalled at Leonard's account of the appointment. The urologist had simply loaded him up with gadgets without bothering to give him a medical examination. The doctor hadn't even asked him any questions about his habits or his health, and Pamela knew that Leonard was taking medications for high blood pressure and sleep issues, as well as antidepressants. He also had a history of smoking.

Gloria and Pamela discussed the disappointing urologist visit but focused more on how Pamela and Leonard had neglected to have an open conversation about their sexual expectations prior to getting intimately involved. Gloria encouraged her to have this conversation. Pamela later reported that they went on to have a loving, mature sexual relationship based on the realities of their age.

Leonard also found a new doctor, who gave him a medication evaluation and reduced his prescriptions by 70 percent.

There can be a time and a place for the sort of interventions Leonard's urologist recommended, and medications like Viagra and Cialis can also help (again, *check with your own doctor first*). None of these will make us twenty-years-old, though, so that leaves the ability to have a frank, honest conversation as the surest way to navigate ED. From what I've seen, this is the biggest factor in determining whether erectile complications make or break a relationship early in those formative stages.

In my practice I have found that by getting away from focusing on erections and beginning to focus on how someone can be a sophisticated lover and practice giving pleasure, a man can have a more satisfying experience. The real answer is to focus on what the renowned sex therapists Virginia E. Johnson and William Masters call the "pleasure bond." The quicker the focus changes from performing to demonstrating love and mutual intimacy, the quicker the problem will be solved, even if that full erection never shows up.

I have a friend named Ed, another retired psychologist, who lost his erection due to prostate surgery and radiation for cancer while in his sixties. He had a direct and honest discussion with his wife about how they could continue their intimacy. They committed to finding ways to be close physically and to express their love for each other, and they went on to learn and experiment with several new techniques that they found to be very enjoyable. (I didn't ask for details, but perhaps he was referring to things like mutual masturbation, oral sex, and "stuffing," which is a technique where the soft penis is used by the woman to stimulate the clitoris and vaginal area.) I was really impressed with how mature he and his wife had been in dealing with the change in their life.

It might not be easy to talk about ED, but whether it occurs due to surgery, radiation, or just with age, it's a necessary conversation. In order to have a loving, physical connection with a partner, both will need to make some decisions together about the best way to go forward. And to the women: if the man in your life does not initiate this conversation, you might need to be the one. Help him by creating a supportive, accepting atmosphere, and be prepared to discuss your expectations without judgment.

 **GLORIA**

For women

All right, ladies—it's our turn! Although men have the lion's share of the burden when it comes to performance, we women can face our own complications as our bodies get older. Vaginal dryness can be an issue, but simple lubricants are an easy solution. Much more complex is our ability to have an orgasm. Some women take the approach of replicating Meg Ryan's famous abilities, as demonstrated in the restaurant scene in the film *When Harry Met Sally*. But faking orgasms really only addresses their partner's ego.

If orgasms are important to you, a savvy and understanding

gynecologist can help. As with men, whatever the struggles or questions might be, you're not alone. We have heard it all, and so have the doctors. At this level of maturity, though, sex can and should be about a whole lot more than the strength of an erection or the ease of having an orgasm.

Senior hearts and minds

Although certain aspects of our bodies' functioning might not be quite the same as they were when we were younger, most of those performance issues primarily affect intercourse, or penetrative sex, which seemed like the end-all and be-all when we were younger. In those earlier years, we were perhaps more susceptible to being pressured into doing things we thought we needed to do to please our partners and keep them around. Our ego needs were much more likely to get in the way, and many of us felt the need to project a certain image to our partners that perhaps did not fit us very well.

At this age, however, we're much more attuned to what we want, and much more able to communicate about it. We can use the wisdom and experience we've accumulated over the years and through our past relationships to explore and find great pleasure in forms of intimacy beyond basic intercourse. And as we've emphasized throughout these chapters, we're evolving into an understanding that this whole process—of dating, partnering, and intimacy—is about finding what works for us and avoiding the things we know we don't want.

Pleasurable, mutual sex begins with connection, and one of the best ways to create connection is through communication. In the prior section, we encouraged conversations about each other's sexual expectations. Not only does such a conversation help to avoid the potential embarrassment of performance issues, but it also builds safety, trust, and closeness, the foundations of intimacy. Talk about what you like and what you want with your partner. Talk about your desires, both in terms of what you like to receive and what you like to provide. When we can be vulnerable about hopes and wants, we give our partners the opportunity to respond in a caring, loving way, which further builds intimacy.

Such conversations can easily shift into what might be called foreplay, but which can also be a full sexual experience in its own right. Kisses and caresses, both focusing on erogenous zones and elsewhere, can convey great love and tenderness. We have heard reports from some clients about the prevalence of the term "cuddling," which can have a variety of meanings. For some clients, it tends to describe holding one another, and perhaps some kissing, but for many, it can refer to everything but full-on intercourse. Whatever it comes to mean for you and your partner, it can be a stimulating and fulfilling experience that does not rely on intercourse or orgasm.

Many of us, when we've been alone for a while (and especially men, in my practice) tend to turn to pornography and masturbation for our sexual needs. There's nothing wrong with this in itself, but as a model for connective, mutual sex, it's sorely lacking in the key areas we're discussing here. So, if this describes you, you might need to work on all the mutual pleasuring skills that pornography skips: conversation, sweet-talking, caresses, and so forth. I have heard stories from a number of my female clients who have dated men who struggled to make this adjustment.

One particularly unfortunate woman, whom I'll call Louise, had encountered multiple men whose idea of sex was to masturbate to pornography in front of her. While mutual masturbation can be exciting and stimulating, she was uninterested in this scenario. It left her wondering, "Who am I to him and why am I even here?" None of these relationships went anywhere. If you're a man in this category, there's help available. Counseling, either individually or with a partner, can help redirect arousal toward a more mutual, satisfying experience.

Although our bodies work a little differently, the wisdom and experience we've got stored in our hearts and minds can go a long way toward contributing to a satisfying and stimulating evening in the bedroom. With vulnerable conversation, attentiveness, and patience, we can please our partners while demonstrating how much we admire and care for them. And while we've heard many stories like the one from Louise, we've heard even more like the one from Alice, who began dating after her marriage of 40 years came to end.

Alice met a man named Pete whom she really liked, and their relationship progressed into the bedroom. Sure enough, she had to acknowledge that she wasn't in her twenties anymore, and neither was Pete. Her body's responsiveness had declined, and Pete's erections were not what they once had been. But she and Pete were both at an age where they had moved past their fears and their expectations, and they were able to communicate and attend to each other in new ways. Alice was surprised and delighted to find that the focus had shifted to mutual pleasuring and a loving, caring interaction. She found the experience to be wonderful, even better than the sex she'd experienced as a younger woman.

Experiences like Alice's and Pete's are out there, regardless of how much our bodies might have changed. The key is to understand that sex is about so much more than intercourse and orgasms. There are many avenues to connective intimacy, and with some openness and some mature conversation, we have every confidence that you'll find ways to keep things both exciting and tender with a new partner.

For men

All right guys, it's time to gather around for a frank conversation about the male approach to sex. Why am I offering men this extra discussion? Because, like it or not, I've observed that we're the ones who are most likely to bring antiquated, unhelpful, egocentric attitudes about sex into these relationships. Remember Louise's story, about all the guys whose idea of a good time was to masturbate to pornography while she, a real-life, interested woman, simply hung around in the periphery? Not once have Gloria or I ever heard of this working the other way around. Women, especially at this age, are often looking to be romanced, to feel cherished. The physical part of the relationship is merely a demonstration of the closeness you feel toward her emotionally and spiritually.

The approach that many took in their twenties isn't going to work. The goal is not to put notches on the headboard, and those men looking for a "wham-bam-thank-you-ma'am" situation are in for some disappointment. And they're likely to anger a number of perfectly wonderful partners along the way.

I had a client once named Jim, who had been single for several years following his divorce. He was on a dating site, but he was rarely able to get past the first or second date before his companions told him they weren't interested. When he came into therapy, he told me that he was never able to "score." As we discussed the situation, a picture began to emerge. He was focused on sex, and his attempts at conversation reflected this preoccupation. The people he tried dating were turned off by his comments and went running for the hills. When I confronted him about this, he was surprised, but in the course of our sessions he realized that his approach to dating hadn't changed since he'd been in his early twenties. As we continued to explore his attitudes, I found out that Jim's father, who had been divorced several times, had no idea how to have an emotionally intimate relationship. This was Jim's role model, so it is no surprise that Jim didn't know how to develop the friendship and loving relationship he so desired.

At this age, sexual intimacy is about companionship, mutual respect, and the goal of making love to your best friend. If those are your goals and some part of Jim's story resonates with you, even a little bit, then one of the first steps is to check your ego. In my practice over the decades, I have found that the male ego can be quite fragile. I've seen many men whose egos couldn't handle it when their date didn't reciprocate their early interest in a sexual relationship. But many people—both women and men—require emotional safety and intimacy before the physical component can be there. So, if you're looking for something serious and lasting, set your ego aside and develop some patience.

Once the ego is out of the way, pay more attention to the needs and desires of your potential partners, which is how to build mutual intimacy. And it's not just about paying attention, but also about asking questions. We're lucky if assumptions are right half the time, but by creating the space for safe conversations, free from pressure, we create the opportunity to respond and accommodate a partner in entirely new ways. This level of consideration is critical to developing the emotional foundation for true intimacy.

As my conversations with Jim went on, he realized he had to change, because he was lonely and wanted a companion in his life. After a number of sessions, I was able to convince him to focus on building friendships, and that this would be the best way to develop an equitable romantic relationship. I told him to try to find mutual interests and be open to a partner's feelings and thoughts. I even coached him to first find out if he even *liked* the whole person before he decided to go to bed—something he'd never really considered before.

These were all big revelations for Jim, and he's not the only one. I've spoken with many other men in the course of my practice who did not have good role models when it came to developing emotional intimacy and had not been able to mature beyond the notches-on-the-headboard phase. But we aren't doomed by our fathers' limitations. We all have the capacity to evolve and mature. Jim did—and with his new approach he was able to find and sustain a relationship where he gives and receives emotional, spiritual, and physical intimacy.

Common questions regarding senior sex

Beyond the issues of physical changes and the expansiveness of the intimate experience at our age, we get asked a whole lot of other questions by clients who have been away from the game for years or even decades. You may have several of your own, and if so, it's important to find answers to continue on the fearless dating journey. This can be a great time to connect with a dating buddy or with someone who has had experience in these areas. If the questions are more involved or personal, a doctor or a therapist can help.

We've compiled a list of some of the more common questions we've come across:

1. When is it appropriate to begin a sexual relationship?

2. Should I be concerned about sexually transmitted diseases?

3. Should we use a condom?

4. Is an invitation to go out of town an obligation to have sex?

5. I had a bad experience with my last partner. How do I handle this?

6. What will others think?

We'll answer them one-by-one, drawing from our own experience, our research, and what we've seen among our friends and clients.

1. When is it appropriate to begin a sexual relationship?

At this point in our lives, sex is no longer for the purpose of making babies. A sexual relationship is for mutual physical pleasure and is a way to indicate the love and affection that a couple share. It should be safe, loving, and mutually agreed upon. There is no time frame other than what feels right to both partners.

Of course, it often happens that this point will be different for different people. If one partner is ready before the other, be patient, and remember that the best sex happens when participants meet each other halfway. If your partner is ready first, and you're feeling pressure, remember that having sex is entirely your choice. As we've said before: this whole adventure is about finding what feels right, so think carefully about spending time and energy on someone who can't give the time and space to your own processes.

One of our clients, Wendy, was dating in her sixties when she came into therapy, disgruntled about the number of men she dated who wanted a sexual connection earlier than she preferred. This is a common dynamic. We have found that men tend to think of sex as a key measure of the woman's acceptance. As Wendy was, women will need to be prepared to handle this particular situation, which may be an important early turning point in a relationship. With some preparation and knowledge, this asymmetry won't derail a promising beginning. Maintain your boundaries and rise above sexual pressure, but if you care about a suitor and are interested in a future, make sure to also communicate your attraction and desire for a connection.

Wendy provided additional insights on intimacy with her account of the time when a partner pressured her for oral sex early in their relationship. This was her first relationship after the death of her husband, and it was very exciting for her. It was a real turn-on, both physically and mentally, to be desired and to feel loved again, and the excitement affected her judgment.

Many of you might relate because it all has to do with neuro-chemistry. There's a small, almond-shaped structure in the brain called the amygdala, which plays heavily into our heightened emotional responses. When we're falling in love, its function changes, and we drop our defenses. Wendy gave in to her partner's pressure, but then found herself regretting her decision, because as time went on, he came to *expect* oral sex, and she became resentful. It became clear how one-sided things were in the bedroom when he brought up sadomasochism and asked her to dress like a cheerleader. She left the relationship to find something more equitable.

In a new relationship, it's important to use common sense and to be wary of going too far out of our own comfort zone. We could be setting ourselves up for unrealistic expectations. Remember, there are other ways to show love and affection, like hugging, kissing, and mutual masturbation, to name a few.

2. Should I be concerned about sexually transmitted diseases?

Later age brings plenty of health complications, and the last thing any of us needs is more! If both parties wish to explore the sexual aspects of the relationship, then it's important to discuss health. And not just a general discussion; we highly suggest trading written assurances from your doctors.

It can be a little daunting to bring this up, but potential partners should be willing to share this information. No one should be offended by being asked. If they are, or if they refuse to provide it, that indicates that they don't respect your needs or your concerns. Health is far more important than the anticipated, brief moment of discomfort when making the request. The right person will see this request as a welcome opportunity to connect with each other.

3. Should we use a condom?

There are two reasons to wear a condom: to prevent pregnancy and to reduce the likelihood of the transmission of STDs. If you're past your fertile years, that knocks out the first reason. And as far as

STDs go, they can still be transmitted through manual or oral stimulation. Condoms, at best, do only a marginal job of protection. (Please see our suggestion regarding Question Two.) With information from a physician, who can also provide up-to-date information about STD transmission and prophylaxis (in other words, the up-to-date tools for disease prevention), each partner can be less worried about STDs.

4. Is an invitation to go out of town an obligation to have sex?
The answer to this is a flat "NO." You are an adult. Only do what you want to do. You're under no obligation to sexually please the other person. If we receive an invitation like this, our company in itself should be *plenty*. If it is not, that tells us something about the relationship.

5. I had a bad experience with my last partner.
How do I handle this?
As we discussed earlier in this chapter, communication is key. We recommend discussing negative experiences early in a relationship, so both partners know what to avoid. This should minimize the chances of repeating the bad experience. These conversations are not always comfortable, but the right partner will be understanding and responsive to clear communications about important likes and dislikes. Tap into your self-awareness and experience and advocate for yourself.

6. What will others think?

Some of us enjoy a good measure of privacy, but others of us are in close communities that might include children (whether adult or otherwise), friends, or neighbors, many of whom might feel the need to keep an eye on us and look out for what they feel are our best interests. Sometimes this can feel invasive, but at other times our friends or family can provide valuable perspective and help us to gauge the suitability of a new person of interest when we might be too close to make those judgments ourselves. Typically, these introductions to new partners aren't made until things are fairly serious, and by then it can be hard to hear critical feedback. Keep an open mind but remember that ultimately, it's about your life, your happiness, and your choices.

 GLORIA

Regardless of who a new partner might be, there are still others who might judge us for engaging in an intimate relationship. In some parts of the country, traditional ideas about gender roles and propriety can still have an effect. Some still see living with a partner as "shacking up". This, in fact, was an accusation that was leveled at me at a recent party, in regard to my relationship with Frank. I wish my late mother had been around to hear it.

When my mother was 78, my dad died after a stroke and a number of years of disability. My mother had been a real caretaker.

Several years after Dad died, she saw an obituary in her local newspaper stating that an old boyfriend's wife had died. She waited a couple of months and called him. They met for lunch, and it was the beginning of a dating relationship. One day she called me in tears to tell me that her boyfriend had mistakenly parked his car in her driveway all night rather than down the street. She said that the neighbor had reported her to their Mormon bishop and that he had called her in for a meeting. She was mortified and surprised when I said, "Good for you! You go, girl!" By the time the call ended, we had replaced her tears with laughter.

If we're concerned about what others think, the first thing to ask is why we care. Perhaps it's to protect ourselves from criticism. If that's the case, we can each develop an understanding of what we need from friends and family. We can seek that out and ignore the rest. On the other hand, if we're more concerned with our reputations or about being a subject of gossip, then ask how much it really matters, and whether those concerns are big enough to prompt a change in behavior. We're the only ones who can answer that question!

Physical intimacy can be messy but it's worth it!

Physical intimacy is a very special development during senior dating. Our clients report many intense moments around their early experiences in the bedroom with their new people of interest. So don't be surprised if it is a little messy—life is messy! But with some preparation and the right attitude, seniors can meet these situations with confidence and wisdom. Be brave and fearless; the rewards can be tremendous, as they were with our client Betty. After the death of her husband of 30 years, Betty became ambivalent regarding online dating until she met a man who "turned her on." She told us that she had not had a sexual relationship for more than five years and that she had forgotten how exciting and satisfying being with a man could be.

Wrap-up

Beyond physical intimacy, of course, there will be many further developments in a relationship. Sometimes these can be big and dramatic, but other times they can be subtle shifts. Sometimes everything will seem like it's going great, and that we've found a keeper, only to have things fall apart. In the next chapter, we will discuss the different stages of a relationship, so you'll be prepared for whatever comes your way.

Journal Questions from Gloria

- What are my sexual expectations?
- How often do I want sex?
- Do I need to have an orgasm?
- Do I need to have penile penetration?

- Is mutual masturbation satisfying enough?
- How interested am I in oral or anal sex?
- Am I ready to have a frank conversation with my partner?
- Are there past poor sexual experiences that I need to resolve or to explore with my current partner?

FRANK

Journal Questions from Frank

- What turns me on, and can I have a conversation with my partner about the same?
- What are my sexual expectations?
- How often do I desire physical pleasuring and what kind?
- Is pillow talk part of our sexual foreplay?
- Can I have a full erection or, a soft erection, or none at all?
- Is mutual masturbation enjoyable and is it enough?
- Am I interested in finding ways to pleasure my partner? (You might have to ask!)
- What are the ways I want a partner to pleasure me?
- Do I like sexual toys and what are they?
- What toys does my partner like?
- Do I like to express my enjoyment during pleasuring and being pleasured by and with my partner?
- Do I like it when my partner expresses pleasure, and do I want to encourage that expression?

Wrap-up

These questions are meant to be a starting point. To learn more, consider reading one of the many books on human sexuality. Over the years we have recommended *The Joy of Sex* by Alex Comfort to many of our clients. We are sure you will have a number of other questions about sexuality including the post-sex reactions and how to protect your heart after sleeping with someone for the first time in many years. There are too many good books on sexuality to present them all. In closing this chapter, then, we'll simply say that it is only natural to make comparisons between sexual partners, and that it takes time to work out a mutually rewarding sexual experience. That being said, exploring our sexuality with a new partner, one we love and respect, can be a fun and exciting experience.

Practice conversation

How might you create a supportive, accepting atmosphere, and discuss any expectations without judgment? Drawing on the previous journal answers, write out the kind conversation you hope to have with a partner about sexual intimacy.

klossher

"FIRST, WE TELL MY SIBLINGS ABOUT US THEN WE WORK ON YOUR CHILDREN FOLLOWED BY A SNEAK VISIT TO MY IN-LAWS. FROM THERE AN ASSAULT ON YOUR UNCLE ..."

CHAPTER SIX

The Four Stages
of a Relationship

We've explored the online services, how to manage those initial contacts, and provided examples of a slew of first dates—and maybe a smattering of second dates. Perhaps someone has emerged and taken hold of your imagination and your heart, and one of those second dates became a third and a fourth. Perhaps you and a partner have navigated those vulnerable first encounters in the bedroom, and now this new love seems as though it might well be here to stay. What happens next?

Relationships are not linear processes. Typically, they go through several stages. Each stage brings its own gratifying pleasures, but also challenges—some of them significant. With some understanding, however, and with courage and a sense of humor, seniors can find their way through them all and settle into that state of deep, intimate partnership, the ultimate expression of true love.

Early in her nursing career, Gloria discovered the work of psychologist Bruce Tuckman, who studied the formation and evolution of social groups. Tuckman proposed four stages of development: forming, storming, norming, and performing. While his work was largely centered on working environments and productivity, we have found that the process of becoming a committed couple follows the same trajectory. We have found that as Frank and I have negotiated our new relationship, an understanding of these stages has helped us to demystify what we have been experiencing as a new couple. We'll share them here so that you, too, will be more prepared to handle changes with grace and patience.

Forming is the first stage: the initial contact, the first date. When things seem like they're likely to go somewhere, the excitement rises, and then the storming phase begins as each partner tries to figure out how this new reality works. The storming stage earns its name because it can be messy and unpredictable. Once through that process, norming occurs: new partners adjust to each other and develop routines, and much of the raw emotion is replaced by calm discussions. Performing is the final stage. A relationship is performing its best when there's respect, safety, equality, understanding, and intimacy between partners—but we don't get there overnight.

In this chapter, we'll go through each stage and share the highs and the lows. We'll offer information on what to savor and what to watch out for, and to illustrate these stages, we'll use a story we know well: our own! We've made our way to that beautiful, peaceful performing stage, but it wasn't always easy. Fortunately, we understood the pressures around us, and we knew how to manage not only our expectations but others' as well. Well, most of the time, anyway...

Read through the following stages and think about past relationships. What might you have done differently if you'd seen this bigger picture? What might you do differently this time?

Forming

The first stage of a relationship is magical. The chemistry is sky-high, and there's a mix of excitement and comfort, as you feel like you have known this new interest forever. This is the stage when couples stay up way too late talking, finding themselves daydreaming constantly about each other when not together. It can be hugely energizing, and a great boost to self-esteem. Who among us wouldn't hold our head a little higher, knowing there's someone out there who has fallen in love with us?

The forming stage begins with that first little glimmer, perhaps noticing each other across a room, or when a standout online profile turns into a lively text exchange. People find themselves waiting for responses to their messages with excitement, and those first couple of dates leave them wanting more and thinking about the possibility that they've just met someone special, perhaps even "The One." Our main piece of advice here is to enjoy it! Falling in love is one of the greatest pleasures life offers, and this stage usually doesn't last long, so savor every moment.

If this is such a magical, beautiful time, what could the downside be? We would caution that it can be easy to get carried away in this stage and to let our guard down. It's an intoxicating stage, but as with any form of intoxication, the brain seals the deal by releasing oxytocin, which is often called "the love hormone." It is a neuropeptide in the hypothalamus secreted by the pituitary gland during times of sexual excitement. This can be as addictive as any street drug. There's a greater likelihood during this excitement phase of making decisions we'll regret in the morning.

It's important to step away from all the breathless excitement and try to see the bigger picture. Does this person of interest have opinions or habits that seem like they could be tough to deal with in the long run? Do you feel like a better person when you're together? We don't just mean do you *feel* better; all that chemistry tends to make us feel like we're walking on air. But in a deeper sense, do they help you become the person you want to be? Is this someone who brings out the best in you? A dating buddy can be especially helpful at this stage. Pay extra attention to their input because they might notice things that we're too lovestruck to see.

 GLORIA

Frank and I first formed a connection on Silver Singles. We exchanged our business web sites and arranged a first meeting at an upscale restaurant in Phoenix. He arrived first, and as I approached the table he stood up and gave me a smile that warmed me. He had a nice, relaxed way of relating, and the chemistry was immediate.

Over dinner we discovered great similarities in our work, our intellects, and our approaches to life. The conversation came easily, as did laughter. By the time the meal was over I knew I'd want to see him again, and soon.

I'd gotten a ride to the restaurant, so he offered to take me home. He made a joke about me stopping by his place to see his "etchings" on the way, and his jaw dropped when I said, "Sure!" He showed me his therapy office as well. He sat in his chair, and I jokingly laid down on his couch. I remember getting a real kick out of my free "therapy session" with this insightful man.

He called the next day, and I told him I was going to pick up my friend at the airport. She was flying in from New York to help me out, as I would be having shoulder surgery in three days. I wasn't too familiar with the Phoenix area or the airport at that time, so he offered to drive me to pick her up. This gave us another hour of lively conversation. I accepted gratefully and together we drove to pick up my visitor, who was a bit surprised at my new boyfriend.

The next day I invited Frank over for dinner and a game of cards, and from that point on he was a constant fixture in my life. The day after surgery he offered to stay with me to help, as I couldn't drive or lift my arm. By then we had spent five days together, and I was totally comfortable being taken care of by this lovely man. He became my primary caregiver, staying with me around the clock. Not only did he help me get around, but he helped me wash my hair and get dressed. I'd never had this sort of care, and it was incredible to be with someone so nurturing. We bonded immediately.

After another week, he began planning outings for us to keep me entertained as I continued to heal. Ten days after we met, we went to Sedona and stayed in a romantic cottage where we discussed being in a committed relationship and maybe getting married. The next day we bought matching rings. It was an absolute whirlwind of a forming stage, but he was 78, and I was 82, and we both knew what we'd found. We wanted to cherish every moment together. I knew I'd found "The One," my soulmate, and we were completely in love with each other. But then it was time to share the news with others, and that's when the storming began.

FRANK

When I met Gloria, I was in the midst of evaluating my life and circumstances and I was just about to give up hope that I would find the love I desired. I'd been in a two-year loveless relationship with an artist I'd met online. She needed a place to do her art and she needed a job, and we'd gotten along well enough in the beginning, so she moved in with me, where she could share my studio and run my practice for a paycheck. Before long we were merely friends, and my career as a psychologist was in its twilight.

She finally decided to move out in search of a new way to pursue her art ambitions. I decided to try my luck online one more time before looking for a senior living situation. Nothing immediately panned out, and a couple of months later I was in the supermarket when I bumped into a woman whom I'd dated a couple of years earlier. She and I began to hang out again, but it was clear this was just another dead end. I was still looking online, but I had again turned my attention to my retirement and a possible move to senior living. I thought what I needed was a quieter, simpler life. How wrong I was!

Then one day I connected online with Gloria. When she sent me the website from her foundation, and I was really excited about meeting someone so accomplished. When I met her, though, I found she was also down-to-earth, and that made a big impression on me. She was relaxed, confident, and really seemed interested in getting to know me and what I was about.

I was stunned when she agreed, after drinks and dinner, to come to my home studio to see my sculptures. I called her the very next day, and she immediately invited me over. Here I was, getting ready to settle down alone, and now, all of a sudden, this woman had landed in the middle of my life, bringing excitement, energy, intelligence, and romance. I did not think that these were going to be a part of my future, but there they were. It was like being reborn and given a new life.

We both had been around the block a time or two and we knew that this was special. We were also aware that our time on Earth was limited. After a couple of weeks, when the topic arose of us committing to each other for the rest of our lives, it was as easy a decision as I've ever made. She was not a solitary entity, however: she had three children and ten grandchildren, and it was time to update them on developments. Enter the storm!

Storming

In Tuckman's model, the next stage, storming, is a phase when the group's structure, power dynamics, and leadership characteristics come under stress, resulting in interpersonal conflicts. The group's energy has to go into resolving these conflicts before the real productivity can begin. In the evolution of relationships, the storming phase is when the focus shifts from the one-to-one relationship to the bigger picture, and how the couple will fit into and relate to the outside world. Of course, it would be nice if everybody could just happily climb aboard the ship of bliss and celebrate this new and wonderful thing in their lives, but alas, there are reasons why in-law jokes have been around for all of history. Sometimes people can have awfully strong opinions about our decisions, whether those opinions are asked for or not.

It is important develop a strong bond before plunging into this stage. We have worked with many couples whose relationships were strained to the limit, and often beyond, when family members didn't approve. Gloria, for instance, had a golfing friend at one point, a woman who was in her late 70s when she fell in love with a man ten years older. Everything seemed like it was going fine but then one day he called her to tell her that his children, although they liked her, had counseled him to break off the relationship. They told him he was "too old" to be dating. She was heartbroken. Shortly after their break-up, he died (from what she believed was a broken heart).

That might be an extreme example, yet we've seen the type of pressure that family members can place upon a new relationship. In fact, Gloria wrote a book called *The In-Law Survival Guide*, which discusses the sort of power the extended family holds. They're in a unique position to either support the couple's ideas wholeheartedly or to challenge them without the sugarcoating they might get from close friends.

But remember: only you have the power to control your life and your relationships, even when your family is moving in a different direction. If your bond is strong and you're resolute in your knowledge of how you feel and why you want this relationship in your life, then you'll be able to weather the storm. There are several things you can do to prepare for the possible backlash.

First, be prepared to stand up for the relationship. Make it clear that you are a couple and that you want to remain a couple, even in the face of outside criticism. Make it clear that you are willing to listen to the family's concerns, but on a limited basis. Tell friends and relatives that you understand they have concerns, but that both partners will determine if things might change, and how. Make it clear—especially to adult children—that they are really important, and that your relationship with them isn't going to end. Remember that many of their attitudes and opinions come from their genuine care and protectiveness.

Be prepared to address questions about important issues like health, healthcare, and money. This means that the couple needs to figure these things out first, of course. They aren't exactly the sexiest conversations to have during that forming phase, so we recommend giving it just a little extra time so that initial excitement can cool down and create space for deeper conversations like these.

It's true that Gloria and I dove into this stage rather quickly; but remember: we'd both had years of psychological training, we'd counseled thousands of people, and we both knew exactly what we wanted. We were also able to have all those conversations early and readily, thanks to our professional experience. So even though it was a breathtaking period, we didn't take shortcuts, and we don't suggest that others do, either.

Finally, find support wherever possible. Be in regular touch with a dating buddy, a therapist, or someone else who will be able to focus on you and your experience without getting caught up in their own fears or concerns. This will help you stay in touch with your own feelings and maintain your boundaries, and it can be a helpful place to strategize about how to manage the more difficult opinions.

This stage can be a lot of work and something of a harsh letdown after that magical forming phase, but it's critical if all these relationships are going to co-exist peacefully. This is important work for your overall happiness, so remember to celebrate the small victories. Ultimately, you're bringing together people whom you love and who love you, and sharing the things you care about the most with the people you care most about. Although it can be a stormy process, the payoff can be huge.

 GLORIA

Frank and I had a very intense forming phase, and our transition into the storming phase was no different. It started one morning, just before I was scheduled to record on Zoom for our podcast *Open to Hope* with my three daughters, Heidi, Rebecca, and Heather. Heidi, my oldest, is the show's co-host, Rebecca handles marketing, and Heather, my youngest, handles the technical aspects. We were to appear together in the recording with our guest for the week. I was at Frank's kitchen table where I had quiet and privacy, as he was in a session with a client in his office. My daughters were scattered around the country at their various homes.

Shortly before recording I was having a text exchange with Rebecca, the second of my three daughters, when I included a piece of news she wasn't quite expecting: I was planning on marrying my new boyfriend. In retrospect, there was probably a better way to break the news to them, but nothing I could have done would have stopped the storm. To say that Rebecca was livid was putting it mildly. She recruited her sisters to confront me about it after our recording session. Somehow, they managed to keep their composure for the recording, but once we wrapped up and our guest left, the clouds broke open.

Rebecca started with the fact that their father—my husband of more than 60 years—had died less than two years earlier, and there was a feeling among them that I was being disloyal. They told me I was being impetuous and childish for marrying a man I'd known for only three weeks. I responded that at my age, I had the right to do anything that I wanted and did not need the permission from my children. I understood their concerns and that, from their perspective, these were all valid criticisms. But they weren't my age, they didn't have my experience, and they weren't *me*. And I told them all as much. It got so heated that Heather went offline for a while, but then Heidi convinced her via text to return to the conversation.

Rebecca continued to chastise me for my bad behavior, demanding to know how I could be so callous as to tell her in a text that I was getting married. By that point I was feeling completely drained, so I just said, "Because I am an asshole." Soon afterward, poor Frank, who had just wrapped up a therapy session, came walking into the kitchen, totally unaware of what was going on. "Here's Frank," I told my lion's den of daughters. "Why don't you talk to him?"

FRANK

I came into the kitchen with no idea what was happening, but a look at Gloria's body language and her daughters' faces on the screen told me what I needed to know. I took a seat next to her and was quickly introduced to each one, and they were looking at their cameras like they'd just seen an armed robber break into their mom's house. Luckily, I was still in therapy mode, so I settled back in my chair and asked the "patient-calming question." I said, "What would you need from me to make you feel comfortable?" This broke the ice, and we began to talk.

Their concern was at the root of our conversation, so it was important that they lead the discussion. They asked questions and Gloria and I calmly tried to answer them, without saying much extra. They wanted to know how Gloria knew I was "The One," and she said it was because we spoke the same language, since we are both psychologists and were of the same generation. She told them that she loved my creativity as a sculptor as well as a therapist, and we reassured them that I was financially responsible. And because I'm four years younger than she is, I'd be able to keep up with her active lifestyle. I think they could see our shared sense of humor, also, and there were some chuckles when Rebecca raised a question about how this would affect Gloria's decisions and independence. I responded by saying, "Rebecca, I can't control your mother!"

As we talked, the conversation continued to settle, and her daughter's initial anxieties abated. Of course, it would take a long time for me to earn their full trust and acceptance, but we were making it through the initial surprise. Gloria conceded that she could have handled the situation in a better way, and we finally signed off on a good note. (The best part of it was that we'd continued recording after the podcast. The whole wild conversation is preserved for posterity, and something we'll be able to laugh about for years to come.)

As we continued to navigate the storm, Gloria and I found our commitment to each other strengthening. It helped clarify all the reasons we were together, and it was an important step in getting to know more about each other and becoming more integrated into each other's lives. If you encounter such a storm, remember that although it isn't as fun as the forming stage, it's just as important, and it's the beginning of the real work that goes into building a lasting, mutual relationship.

It can sting when someone calls a new partner into question but try not to take it personally. Their doubts reflect their own fears, not your judgment. Try to see the situation from their point of view and allow space for them to adjust to the new developments. And finally, don't try to defend yourself or your partner. We tend to overreact when we're feeling accused, and this often just leads to more conflict. You aren't on trial, and you're not going to change anyone's mind with a speech. Answer their questions, but remember, you don't need anyone's permission to be happy.

Be aware that the storming stage can last a while. Ours was on fast-forward: we had all of Gloria's daughters assembled at once, so they each had a chance to voice their concerns. I have two stepdaughters from a previous marriage with whom I have a great relationship, but with no biological children of my own we didn't have to overcome a similar chorus of disapproval on my side. You might have a more drawn-out process while everyone takes their turn asking questions and figuring out what they need to know to accept things. Keep at it with patience and understanding and recognize how this stage, though sometimes difficult, is strengthening the new relationship.

Norming

When the storm passes, relationships settle into the norming stage, when discussions are calmer and emotions are less raw, when routines and expectations of each other stabilize. The goal of this stage is to uncover what does and does not work for you as a couple. You'll figure out what you like to do on weekends, how often to see friends and family, and how to spend the holidays.

There will also be a million small things to negotiate, too. Who will use which drawer in the bedroom? Who will empty the dishwasher? Who does the wash? Who shops for food and cooks? How often do you eat out? Who pays the bills? What time do you like to wake up and go to bed, and how often do you want to be intimate? If you don't live together, how often will you see each other?

GLORIA

A big goal of this stage is constructing a shared history. Consider taking a class together, going to the movies, planning an adventure, going for walks, or doing something new. Frank is learning to play golf and I am learning to play pickleball. We wrote a book together and are in the process of refining and promoting it.

Keep things in perspective while developing shared experiences. Gratitude and humor can go a long way. Maintain a sense of gratitude at finding one another and stay connected to your sense of humor; these two alone will help with getting through tough times. They will also help each partner to compromise, which is a big part of the norming phase. You should have already figured out the big deal-breakers, of course, those major political, religious, health, alcohol, sexual, and financial issues that make people incompatible. But when it comes to more everyday matters, no relationship will succeed without negotiation. So, take a step back in your own mind and decide what you can and cannot tolerate. Start with a simple baseline: is just being together in the evening enough? Or do you need more? If so, what?

FRANK

Our baseline is that we are in a committed relationship, and we won't be seeing other people. We want to live and sleep together, and we would like to have each other around most evenings. We are open to having time apart if one or the other of us wants to travel. For instance, Gloria had planned a trip to India before we got together, and I decided not to join her and her family on the trip. She travelled as planned, and not only did she thoroughly enjoy the trip, but it also reassured her family that her new relationship with me wouldn't change her family connection.

With a baseline established, the norming period can be a beautiful time of developing a shared history and creating depth and substance beneath the passion. We refer to this as the "Becoming Us" period. We moved in together and spent our time remodeling a home, playing golf, giving dinner parties, going on trips to Europe and Africa, playing cards with Gloria's relatives, and taking pickleball lessons. We have lots of pictures of our time together and for Christmas, Gloria's daughter Heidi gave us several framed pictures and made two picture books of our adventures.

It has been a lot of fun, but it has also been a period of growth and learning. When the prospect of the Africa trip arose, I had doubts that I could make it, since I'd needed a knee replacement for years. But Gloria, who had been there before, was patient and encouraged me to go. She assured me that I could opt out of any activities that would be a problem. She was right—I had a great trip!

Through the norming stage we've learned so much about each other, and about the third entity called "us." We've learned what works and what doesn't, and we've learned how to be together and when to seek our own space. It has been an intense time of bonding, a payoff for the hard work of the previous stages.

Performing

Performing is the fourth and final stage of relationship building, when partners really relax into couplehood and know what to expect. As a couple you've tried a number of things and figured out what works and what doesn't, what to keep and what to let go. You've developed a significant shared history and are enjoying building more. You have inside jokes, your own references, and the small things that arise are easily dealt with.

Performing has been our favorite stage, and today we're really enjoying becoming a family and adding to our shared history.

There are clear indicators of how far we've come from those early days of forming and norming. At a recent birthday gathering, we all sat around and laughed at the shared experience of "the great Zoom storm." The laughter and lightheartedness were beautiful affirmations that Frank had been accepted by Gloria's daughters and that he had become a part of the family. (We even plan to replay the recording sometime for its comedic value.)

We have a shared history, and we can reflect back on these memories and experiences. We can recall the good times like, "Remember when we took the Queen Mary to London?" "Remember when Heidi bought herself that crown and sash for her birthday party?" It's fun to look back on the good times, of course, but surviving tough times together can be an even more powerful factor in bonding.

When we had been together just four months, Frank passed out on the golf course and ended up having a stent put in one of his coronary arteries. It shook us, as we were wondering what the damage would be not only to his health but to our relationship. Luckily the surgery was highly successful and there were no lasting effects to his heart or his brain. Today, we can look back at the photos, which tell the growing story of our time together.

Today, we're also doing things that make us both happy and looking for new ways to keep the passion in our relationship. We're finding ways to create our own rituals and culture. For our first Christmas together, we decided to shake things up and not to have a tree. We didn't want to bother getting out the old ornaments or other decorations. Frank had a childhood memory of fabricating a snowman structure with his father from chicken wire and cotton, so he decided to build something similar for our living room, and that's where we put our presents. Gloria was used to big family gatherings for Christmas, but now her daughters are all in different states, so we gathered for a time on Zoom. It was an understated holiday and we both enjoyed it very much.

It's important to accept change, to embrace the new rituals and routines that you'll create as a couple. Stay curious and flexible and focus on building a new present and future without dwelling on the past. You are part of a beautiful new entity now, and it will take on its own life and become something so much greater than the sum of its parts.

Wrap-up

As with the process of dating, the work of a committed relationship never stops. The performing stage is the ultimate goal, where couples feel calm, supported, and loved, and can focus on what unity can bring not only to the partners but to the people around them. Then, though, there's no guarantee the couple will perform forever. It's possible to backtrack to earlier stages as new events and people enter their lives, creating the need for adjustments. In fact, the dynamic nature of life makes it more likely than not. If we can recognize the stages and know what to expect, we'll be better prepared to handle the unique challenges that come along with each one. We'll have more patience for ourselves and our partners and for the processes going on around us.

Some challenges, however, are bigger than others. In our experience as therapists, we've seen many relationships fall apart, including those that once seemed as strong and stable as they could be. In the next chapter, we'll take a deeper look at what we call "almost experiences": those relationships that don't quite go the distance.

Journal questions

Think about your last partner and consider the four phases of a meaningful relationship.

- What were some of the challenges that arose in each phase?
- How will you navigate those challenges going forward?

Practice conversation

Visualize being in the norming phase, hashing out who will do the dishes, who cooks, etc. Remind yourself of the life you pictured in Chapter One and write out a conversation you plan to have with your partner about routines.

"THIS IS JEANINE. SHE GETS ALL MY CULTURAL REFERENCES."

"AFTER SEVERAL FAILED RELATIONSHIPS I'VE
DECIDED TO START DATING MY SUPPORT GROUP."

CHAPTER SEVEN

When Love Does Not Endure

For every happy, committed, enduring relationship are many that were not designed to go the full distance. Except for those very lucky few of us who meet our first loves and stay together for life, we've all experienced heartbreak at one point or another. We call these "almost experiences." We gave it our all, and it isn't so much that the relationship *failed*. From our perspective, it's more the case that we *almost* found "The One."

Nothing we can say here will take away the sting of a relationship's conclusion, especially when you had high hopes. There are some things that can make recovery from a breakup faster and less painful and might help you prepare to get back out there and back to the search, which is the only way to find the love you're looking for. Stay with it—we believe that you can succeed! Remember: you often have to kiss a lot of frogs before you find a prince.

 # GLORIA

It is very common for an early meet-up, even a promising one, to fail to develop into the love of your life. I myself was with another partner before I met Frank. I felt bad when that relationship ended but I later realized that the opportunity for real success often comes after a failed relationship. I came to see that the dating process is a learning experience. It's a graduate degree in relationships and self-discovery. Frank had multiple marriages for a total of 35 married years, and he had other long-term relationships before he met me, so he was even more of a veteran of relationships. In fact, just prior to meeting me, he was contacted by a past partner who said that she would like to start dating again. Now he's glad that we connected online and that he didn't settle for what he felt was less.

If a relationship is not the right fit, it can hurt but can also clear space for the right one to appear. In this chapter, we will begin with an introduction to some ideas and concepts to help understand the dynamics of those relationships that aren't built for the long haul.

- "Almost experience": A relationship that ends by divorce or break-up.
- Leaver: The person who decides to end the relationship.

- Leavee: The person who is left in the relationship.
- Traumatic "almost experience": An "almost experience" that leaves one partner or both with prolonged emotional or psychological issues such as anger, grief, or feelings of abandonment.
- Positive reframe: a technique from Cognitive Behavior Therapy (CBT) where negative or challenging situations are considered and defined in a more positive way.

The "almost experience"

We've all experienced this—sometimes many times over: an early attraction that couldn't stand the test of time. The initial attraction could be based on physical or mental compatibilities or even just common interests. Before meeting Frank, Gloria, an avid golfer, had a relationship with a man she was attracted to because he was a scratch golfer. Before meeting Gloria, Frank, who is a sculptor, had an "almost experience" with a woman he was attracted to because she was a painter. For a while, she and Frank lived and worked in his home studio. As time went on, though, both of these relationships became "almost experiences," and those common interests alone just weren't enough to serve as the foundations for true, lasting relationships.

Discovering that a relationship isn't going to make the distance is painful for the Leaver and the Leavee. For the Leavee, it can sometimes come as a major surprise. It might seem like everything is going just fine, but then they discover their partner is having a very different experience. It's disorienting and confusing.

It can be just as hard for the Leaver. Although they might have had more time to consider and reflect on the relationship and how it isn't working for them, they once had the same high hopes and dreams. For them, it's a different process, but the transition is the same, from hope and joy to the sad conclusion that this just wasn't true, lasting love. For the Leaver, it can also be very difficult to distinguish between a series of everyday disagreements and true, deepdown incompatibility. Even the happiest couples experience strife and tension—those are to be expected. At a certain point, though, we might come to the difficult decision that the relationship we've been working so hard to maintain might not be the right one. That point can be very difficult to identify.

Remember our realtor, Sandra, for whom we've been acting as dating buddies? At one point, she met and dated a man we'll call Bob, who was also an author and an expert on anxiety disorders. She was impressed by his stature in the medical community and his interest in her own history of anxiety. His career took him around the world constantly, to various events and speaking engagements, and he was only able to see her on occasional weekends. She didn't like the irregularity; but she loved his mind, and she was flattered by his interest in her, and she wanted the relationship to go further. So, she resigned herself to his schedule, and tried to tell herself it would change someday. Then late one fall day when she reached out to him, looking for some company for the holidays, he said that he was just too busy to see her but would contact her in a couple of months. That didn't work for her. Despite their connection, a partner she could barely spend time with didn't feel like a partner at all.

Sandra came to us to discuss it and after thinking it over, she realized what a gift the relationship had been to her. It taught her what she'd been missing and what she wanted, and she became fully committed to finding a lasting relationship that would meet her needs. And although she had first felt a sense of abandonment, which led her to see herself as the Leavee, she evolved to think of herself as the Leaver. She had made the decision to exit the relationship so that she could search for a more available partner.

We were both impressed at how quickly Sandra made this mental adjustment. This is one of the advantages that come with the wisdom of maturity: rather than focusing on what had been lost or what might have been, she focused on her own growth. Sandra was ready to stay in the game as a more competent player, and that's when she engaged the help of the matchmaking service to help her find someone who would better meet her relationship needs.

On the other hand, we've heard many stories from clients who settle for less than they deserve, so when we see signs of this, we get concerned. These less-than relationships can go on and on for years. This can happen to both men and women, but what we see most often are women who hang on to relationships with men who are not willing or able to commit. A common factor in many of these stories is the man who is going to leave his failing marriage to be with his true love—except he never quite gets around to it. Beware of the ones who never get around to divorcing!

Such was the case with a lovely, energetic accountant we met while we were considering the purchase of a condo. Alex met us at the condo with her dog Noodles. She looked to be in her late fifties, and she was athletic and attractive in jeans and a sweater. As we looked around the condo, we mentioned to her that we were doing a book on mature dating. She told us that she had met a man online and had been dating him on an occasional basis for the last two years. She was becoming very disillusioned, though, as he often canceled dates and weekend plans. She then told us that he'd been telling her that he was in the midst of getting a divorce and had only stayed married in order to keep his estranged wife on his health insurance. When she pressed him for a timetable on the divorce, there was never a direct answer. She was still hoping things would end up going her way.

People like Alex can waste a lot of energy and time waiting for a partner to make them a priority. If you want to be a priority, don't settle for anything less. If someone is unwilling to make a real commitment, they're not a good candidate for an ongoing relationship. If they're unavailable, they might be suited only for casual, occasional dating, whether they realize it or not. Waiting around for someone like that to change their mind is likely to be a big waste of time.

Beginning again

In our contacts with people in counseling, we have found that clients who have these "almost experiences" continue to gain competence with every try. They learn through their attempts that there are possibilities out there, and they learn more about what they want and what they don't want. They also report having fun and learning new things about themselves, especially those who have dating support buddies.

So, while there can be a real sting to these endings, don't get stuck in discouragement if you thought that you had found a real keeper, only to find out that it was an "almost experience." You are becoming a seasoned dater and gaining the skills for future attempts with a fresh perspective. Once that sting wears off and you're able to take a step back, ask:

- What was missing?
- What was it that kept you from committing, or that kept the other person from committing?
- Just as importantly, what *did* work?
- What did you get right?
- What would you do again?

In order to become a better dating consumer, use the answers to keep learning about what you do and don't want. As we discussed in Chapter One, the most important learning is to know what you need and want. At the end of this chapter, we invite you as a seasoned dater to again look at what you desire in a partner.

Traumatic "almost experiences"

Sometimes, however, you're *not* ready, because all broken hearts are not created equally. Some heal after a few good cries, some late-night music-and-wine sessions, the support of friends, and perhaps a new hobby. Others don't heal so easily, though, and the Leavee can find themselves struggling with prolonged bouts of anger, grief, depression, and a sense of abandonment—lasting trauma, in other words. For many people, the experiences of their previous relationships can make it really difficult to maintain hope and openness when it comes to love. We've seen this repeatedly among our clients: painful endings lead to fear of rejection or failure, which lead to the acceptance of a lesser option. Consider John's case.

 # GLORIA

As I was jogging down University Avenue in Palo Alto on a sunny Sunday morning, I noticed a young couple who were friends of mine. They were sitting at a small table outside a café with a handsome, well-groomed man of about 65, who had a cup of cappuccino in front of him. They introduced me to their friend John and asked me how Frank and I were progressing on our new book.

"Great," I said. "It's coming along nicely."

"What is your book about?" John asked.

"It's about senior dating," I said, at which point he gave me a sly grin and threw up his hands.

"I'm divorced, and I'll never date or marry again," he said, rather sarcastically.

"Aren't you lonely?" I asked him.

"No," he said. "I fight loneliness by coming to this coffee shop, and I have the perfect woman that I don't have to live with but is always available on demand."

This got me curious. "How does that work?" I asked. "Is she married, and are you waiting for her husband to die?" Laughter rose around the table.

"No," John said. "She's available whenever I need her—she's the woman in my dreams."

I'd heard this, or a version of this, several times as a therapist. John had created a no-risk option for himself, a fantasy that he could use to escape loneliness for brief spells. I felt sympathy for whatever had brought him to this point, but I also thought I might be able to shake him up a little bit and encourage him to think about things a little differently.

"Good luck with that," I said. "I like a real person in my bed, personally." I smiled and continued my jog.

Whatever happened in John's divorce had made him leery of all intimacy, so much so that he'd given up on it entirely, even though he might have decades of life remaining. I wonder how many people are like John, sitting with their cappuccinos, feeling lonely, but settling for fantasy rather than taking a risk? No matter how shocking or surprising your "almost experience" might have been, there are ways to address it and overcome it, to keep going, to keep putting forth the effort, and to refuse to settle for anything less than deep companionship.

Recognize the signs

How do you know if you're in the process of healing from a broken heart, or if you're grappling with trauma? In the beginning, the processes often look pretty similar, so the answer lies in how we bounce back over time. Obviously, the longer and the more intense the relationship, the harder the recovery process will be. A thirty-year marriage, for example, is a whole lot more to grieve than a six-month fling. The circumstances around the breakup matter, too: was it a mutual, respectful parting of ways, or did you discover that someone you thought you knew and trusted was not who they seemed?

In the worst of cases, it can take several months for feelings of acute pain and loss to diminish. After a very difficult divorce or split, give yourself a few months (or more), and then check in on how you're doing. If you're still constantly thinking about the loss, and especially if those thoughts come to interfere with work, self-care, other relationships, or any aspects of your everyday routine, then you're probably dealing with trauma. Lasting troubles with sleeping or eating and weight loss or gain are common in these situations. Even when that period of distress passes and things settle down, you might still be operating from a place of trauma (like John) if you find that your whole outlook on love and dating has shifted significantly.

When we encounter a client whom we feel is at risk for lasting effects, we conduct a relationship assessment to discover the history and nature of the relationship and the attitudes surrounding the separation. We look at the length of the relationship, the degree of intimacy, and the identities of the Leaver and Leavee. Because a Leaver typically has more time to consider the relationship's shortcomings and to justify their decision, they're much less likely than a Leavee to find the separation traumatic.

This might seem obvious, but it isn't as straightforward as it might look on the surface. Some people are not able to summon the responsibility required to end a relationship themselves, so instead they'll behave horribly in order to try to get the other person to leave. Every therapist can relate dozens of these death-by-sabotage relationship stories.

Even without terrible behavior, there can be other, more nuanced differences that can change the typical experiences of the Leaver and the Leavee. The processes of readjusting to life after a relationship and getting over a partner are rarely linear, which can cause the roles to shift. Consider the case of Olivia and Ray, who met in a grief group four months after their respective spouses died, in each case after many years of marriage. Ray was determined to get into a new relationship quickly. His wife had died after years of decline due to Alzheimer's, so he had been feeling alone for years, and he was anxious to start a new life after years of caregiving.

After only a few weeks of dating, he asked Olivia if she would move in with him. She was surprised but agreed. After six months of living together, Olivia took a Christmas trip with her children, and she also included Ray. After a week, Ray was ready to return but Olivia made plans to stay a week longer with friends. This angered Ray, and he returned home alone. During her extended stay she received a text from him stating, "I have decided that our relationship isn't working out for me. Could you pack your things and leave the key to my house on the counter?"

Ray's decision blindsided Olivia, and she was devastated. In therapy, though, she quickly discovered that Ray had been a transitional relationship for her. This helped her to view the trauma differently. Rather than experiencing Ray's actions as abandonment, she was able to reframe the experience. She came to understand that they'd both been in early grief, feeling lonely and abandoned, and neither of them had been ready to make the kind of commitment that they'd made to each other.

As she continued to reflect, she realized there were things that she did not like about the relationship, such as Ray's attitude about money. She acknowledged that it was probably just a matter of time before she would have decided to end the relationship herself. This taught her more about what she wanted in a permanent relationship, and she was able to see that time with Ray had helped her learn more about her needs. With this understanding, and with my encouragement, she signed up for an online dating service and crafted a profile that emphasized her commitment to her family and friends and her need for independence.

Before long she met a man named Mark, who was everything she was looking for. When Ray called her a few months later and asked if they could get back together, she informed him that she was not interested. The Leavee had become the Leaver.

Recovering from a traumatic "almost experience"

Olivia's turnaround was fast and thorough. She'd been with Ray only a matter of months, and she had the perspective to understand that she'd rushed into things. On the other hand, John (whom we mentioned earlier) had experienced something so painful that it had seriously altered his feelings about love and couplehood. Most of us fall somewhere in between. All along that spectrum, though, break-ups and divorces can entail complicated grieving processes.

The dissolution of a long-term relationship often includes a number of factors that can draw out the process. Co-parenting, home ownership, and financial entanglements can keep exes in each other's lives long after the initial split, re-enacting their troubled dynamics and re-triggering trauma. Social media can also draw out the process. Even if you don't follow your ex on Facebook or Instagram, for example, children or other family members might. We've heard stories from our clients about comments and reminders on these platforms that are very hurtful.

Such was the case with Jean, who had three grown children when her husband, Bradley, left her for a younger woman. He said that he needed to start a "new life" as he was no longer happy in the "old life." Turning 60 had been a trauma for him and he felt it was time to "break out and really live." He planned on spending his days rock climbing and skiing while avoiding the "drudgery" of work and family. Unfortunately for the family, he was also a great fan of social media and constantly posted photos of his adventures and his new life and love.

Without telling his children or parents, he and his girlfriend eloped to Las Vegas and posted pictures of their marriage. These reminders kept Jean from being able to process her grief and anger. Each time she was ready to move forward, something else would come up to enrage her again, and she'd find herself back at the beginning. Being the wise woman that she is, she joined a divorce support group and over time was able to move on and develop a new relationship.

Our clients also tell us that there is often far less support for a divorce or break-up than there is after a death. A person's death brings about a more final ending. It's often also a community event, in that every culture has rituals and ceremonies that follow death, which help the survivors to move on. Divorce, however, is seen as a much more private occurrence, but it can result in just as strong a sense of loss and just as much loneliness. As in Jean's story, support groups can be a great way to find community and to keep progressing.

If you've been through an "almost experience" and you're continuing to experience stress, anxiety, and social withdrawal, then we urge you to get help with processing the loss and grief. This is important because Leavees, particularly women, often respond to the separation with a deluge of self-criticism. They can torture themselves with questions: am I too old? Am I too fat? Too thin? Am I too independent? Do I come across as aloof? Am I too dependent? Do I seem clingy? These questions can lead to a worsening spiral that only prolongs the grief process. If you find yourself tipping into this sort of questioning, or otherwise struggling to manage the fallout from an "almost experience," there are ways to help move through the grief process.

The first step is to take a close look at the story you're telling yourself. If that story is keeping you stuck in the past or mired in feelings of depression and withdrawal, then your task is to work to change that. Next, it's important to acknowledge the loss and the impact it's having. Have empathy for yourself—a difficult ending to a relationship can be a big blow to self-esteem, which can cause other problems. This is another place where a dating buddy can be a lifesaver.

Receiving validation for your pain and loss from someone on the outside can go a long way toward removing some of the confusion and illuminating a pathway ahead for healing. A dating buddy can also help to remind you of all the other parts of life: everything you do and everything you are that has helped you to persevere through all the ups and downs. The pain of an "almost experience" can be overwhelming at first, but it doesn't have to define you.

We also advise our clients to journal regularly to combat negative self-talk and to release feelings of abandonment and pain. This practice can be helpful to address and explore questions like, "What did I do to contribute to this?" "Am I not good enough?" "What could I have done differently?" It is equally important to consider what you did right, what you learned, and what you'd choose to do again. Many of our clients find that regular journaling can help them move through these concerns.

If you've ever asked yourself these questions, please know that you did not cause the relationship to end. You are good enough. Things just happen, and we may never know the reasons why. There *is* something you can do differently, though: you can find someone who will love and cherish you.

In addition to talking with friends and journaling, a good therapist can provide valuable perspective and additional strategies for healing. If you decide on therapy, some topics to explore might be your progress through the stages of grief or any lasting anxieties about relationships, intimacy, or vulnerability. Also, revisit the topic of anxiety in Chapter Two and think about your relationship fears in light of this new understanding of your own history of "almost experiences." There can be a close relationship between trauma and one's progression through the stages of grief, so understanding that process can be illuminating. We'll cover the grieving process further in Chapter Nine.

Positive reframing

Positive reframing is a technique used in Cognitive Behavioral Therapy (CBT) to keep potentially devastating experiences from becoming so. In our sadness we can take a normal experience and use it to make the situation worse. When we make a situation seem worse than it is, we tend to make decisions that are not in our best interest. Failure often ensues, and stress around our perceptions of failure can cause further unhappiness.

Reframing the experience can change this and normalize the situation. It can help us see the experience in a true and more helpful light, which can lead to growth. Sometimes this difference can result from just a small tweak in our thinking. Such was the case with Henry.

Henry, a sixty-five-year-old lawyer, had an "almost experience" that brought him into counseling. He had met Jill, a sixty-year-old divorcee whose husband had been a successful banker. Jill was used to a certain lifestyle in her marriage and at first seemed to be happy dating Henry. Henry's law practice was not as successful as he had hoped, though, and as time went on, he found himself unable to keep up with Jill's lifestyle. This caused tension between them, as he was not able to afford the expensive meals and travel to which she had been accustomed. Jill finally said she did not want to see Henry in the future, as their lifestyles were too different. This crushed Henry, and he went into a depression that made his professional work even harder.

In counseling, Henry was able to see that he had known, going into the relationship with Jill, that his financial situation was quite different than hers. He had hoped she would love him enough that the difference would not be a factor. Unfortunately, this wasn't the case, and the sting of the rejection lasted several months. But as time went on and he stuck with counseling, talking with friends, and journaling about what had happened, he began to turn things around. He eventually was able to reframe the whole relationship as a valuable learning experience.

"I thought that I could make her love me enough that money would not make a difference," he said. "I won't make that mistake again. I will find someone that loves me for who I am, not what I have." This gave him the confidence and the direction to go forward, and when he felt he had healed enough to try again, he went online in search of a more appropriate partner. He met a nurse who had a compatible lifestyle. This relationship was more successful, and they were married a year after he discontinued counseling.

Wrap-up

Henry and Olivia are great examples of people who used a variety of techniques to reframe their stories and come out on the other side wiser and more able to find someone who would meet their needs. Anyone can do this with the right knowledge. You have the power to define experiences any way you want, and the consequences of that definition can have an enormous impact on your life.

So, if you have had an "almost experience," we would like to congratulate you on this new opportunity. You've survived the pain and shock that comes with these experiences, and now your courageous vulnerability has given new insight into how to have a better relationship. You've been through feelings of shame and doubt and are still in the game.

It's now time to hone your dating profile using what you've learned, making sure to provide the most accurate picture of the person you are and all your needs and wants. This might mean a new photo that shows you in an activity that will entice a person with a similar interest. It might be a statement about a music preference, a dining preference, or a travel preference that brings interest to the profile. To keep things fresh, you might try a different online service. It's time to make things fun again!

In the final section of this book, we'll explore the relationship problems and issues that often arise in committed relationships. We hope that these closing chapters will help you understand and nurture the right connections, so that a promising start can evolve into a long-term partnership, rather than ending as an "almost experience."

Journal questions

After an "almost experience," it's a perfect time to go back to Chapter One and, with this new experience and knowledge, to refresh yourself on the fundamentals of dating. Make a new profile after answering the following questions:

- What do I want in a partner?
- What do I need to avoid?
- What did I do right in the relationship?
- What would I do differently?
- How far am I willing to go for a meet-up?

Practice conversation

What did the last relationship teach you? Visualize a conversation with a future partner. Tell them what you've learned and ask your future partner what they've learned in their past relationships.

"YOU SHOULD BE HONORED, IT'S NOT EVERYONE
I ASK FOR A DNA SAMPLE ON THE FIRST DATE."

PART THREE

Relationship Challenges

"HE LIKED RELATIONSHIPS, HE DIDN'T LIKE INTIMACY."

CHAPTER EIGHT

Facing Relationship Issues

Each romance is a unique story, but developing senior relationships can pose a number of special issues and challenges not typically seen in the earlier years. These issues can test a couple's passion and commitment, but they also bring opportunities for growth and bonding. In our years as therapists, working with hundreds of couples, we've seen the recurrence of many of these issues. We've seen various approaches to solving them, and we've seen some of these approaches work while others have failed. In this chapter, we'll share some of the most common problems our clients have faced so you'll be ready for much of what might arise. Patience, understanding, communication, and a bit of preparation can help to address these issues and keep a relationship moving forward.

Honest communication is a must

We're starting here because open, honest communication is the basis for resolving anything you might come up against. All relationships are full of negotiations and compromise, but you'll only arrive at that satisfactory middle ground if you speak up for yourself and directly communicate your needs. This isn't always easy—we're all familiar with the way it feels to break bad news to somebody or to give them an answer they don't want to hear. It might be easier in the short term to keep things to yourself, to placate people, make sacrifices, or defer bad news until later, but this is a recipe for resentment, and it doesn't take a whole lot of resentment to put some serious cracks in a relationship's foundation. We've also seen many situations among our clients where the fear of a conversation was much worse than the actual conversation.

One of our clients, Anne, had been in a relationship with Bill for two months when it came time for her to have a hip replacement. Bill offered to come and stay with her for as long as she needed help with recovery, and though she was grateful for his thoughtfulness, she wasn't ready to have him in her home around the clock. She also did not feel that she would have been able to provide the same care for him if their roles had been reversed, and she was wary about creating unrealistic expectations. But she was worried that he might be offended, so she was considering agreeing to his assistance.

We spoke to her about the importance of having an honest conversation with him about caregiving, and she agreed. When she came back to tell us about it, she said that Bill had actually breathed a sigh of relief when she told him she was uncomfortable having him involved in her care. As it turned out, he'd only made the offer out of a sense of duty and obligation. It was not because he wanted to, or even because he thought he'd be good at it. Their frank conversation gave them the opportunity to discuss other possibilities together and develop a plan. Anne hired a night caregiver and arranged a daytime visitation schedule for friends and family who had expressed a desire to help out. Bill visited her daily to provide moral support and they continued their relationship, reading together and binging on *Game of Thrones*.

Your place, mine, or both?

Once in a committed relationship, the question of living together will eventually arise. Some couples choose to continue living separately, preferring to maintain their own spaces. Others will choose to move in together, which can bring financial benefits and increased time with each other. It can be a difficult decision, so we suggest weighing the desire to spend more time together against how much you value your alone time. The question can be complicated if you're not on the same page.

One person may be ready for cohabitation before the other. If you're in this situation, please refer to the earlier section on honest communication! State what you want and why but leave plenty of space for your partner's feelings. Applying pressure out of impatience means creating a recipe for conflict and resentment. Moving in together will create a whole new period of storming and norming (see Chapter Six) as you adjust to the new arrangement, and you'll both need to be equally committed to the process if it is to go smoothly.

If you do decide to live together, of course, the next question is: where? Will you live at your place, at your partner's place, or will you find a new home somewhere together? What if you live in different towns, or even different states?

FRANK

We wanted to spend as much time as possible with each other, so we decided early on to live together. It was an easy choice for us, as we both wanted the same thing. We did face other complications, though, in that Gloria's place was in northern California, while mine was in Arizona.

She was game to move in with me, but decided to keep her home in California, which had been a longtime hub for her family. This would give us two home bases to choose from, and we could go back and forth as needed. But we had another problem to solve. When the question of living together first came up, she came to visit me in my home, which was also my sculpture gallery. She took a look around and commented that with all my art, there wouldn't be much room for her. We decided to find a new gallery for my sculptures, sell the property, and move to a new home that suited both of us. These might have been difficult transitions for someone else, but we were both truly ready to make these changes in our lives to accommodate this new and wondrous relationship. Figuring it all out and planning our future became a big part of the fun for us. We have enjoyed building our new nest together, and we wish the same for you when the time is right.

To marry or not?

At this age, marriage means something a whole lot different than it did when we were in our twenties and thirties. For many young couples, marriage is a big step on the road toward starting a family and otherwise building a life that looks like the traditional ideal: a spouse, perhaps a couple of kids, the white picket fence, and so on. But in the later stages of life, marriage means something rather different. While marriage can retain a lot of its romance and its symbolism, it has big potential implications for finances, healthcare, the estates, and a number of other things. It's a legal contract, a binding agreement that can bring about significant changes, so do some careful research and have some dedicated discussions about what these changes might mean.

Don't get us wrong. We don't mean to reduce marriage to a mere bit of legal paperwork. Regardless of what a lawyer or financial planner might advise, remember that marriage is a personal decision, and there can be many different reasons to tie the knot. Maybe your first wedding (and/or the marriage that followed it!) left something to be desired, and you're looking to replace that story with a new and better one. On an episode of our podcast, we interviewed Jill Johnson-Young, author of the book *The Rebellious Widow: A Practical Guide to Love and Life After Loss*. Jill, who had been widowed twice and was in her third marriage, had been a major advocate for gay marriage and had felt compelled to exercise the right that she had fought so long and hard for.

GLORIA

I'm something of a traditionalist, so when Frank and I fell in love and decided to move in together, I figured that getting married was of course the thing to do. I didn't want to set a poor example for my grandchildren, and I also wondered what my friends would think. But when the dust settled after the big Zoom announcement we made to my daughters, Frank and I sat down to really research the question. We talked to our lawyers, accountants, investment advisors, family, and friends, and we talked about the experiences we'd seen our clients go through. We took a number of preliminary steps, such as drawing up a prenuptial agreement and obtaining a marriage license, but ultimately, we decided to put the wedding on hold. We weren't quite ready for the financial and legal changes that marriage would introduce. The decision to hold off has little bearing on the life we live or the love we share, and the knowledge we gained through our research will make it an easy topic to re-visit in the future.

Caregiving

Although we'd all love our relationships to revolve around romantic dinners, warm days at play, and exciting travel plans, we're not getting any younger, and the questions of healthcare and caretaking loom larger and larger with each passing decade. These topics are a lot less fun, but they're critical to a lasting, thriving relationship. There are a number of different angles to consider here, but the first you're likely to encounter is caregiving after a surgery or an acute illness.

It's important to know just where you stand on caregiving. What are you comfortable providing? What are you comfortable receiving? Don't wait for a broken hip or a heart attack to create the need for this conversation; it's best to have it ahead of time, in a time of health, when you won't feel the pressure from an impending procedure. Be honest with yourself and your partner. Caregiver burnout is very real and can have lasting effects. You can avoid it and protect your relationship by understanding your own abilities and limitations and making sure your partner does too.

I had shoulder surgery shortly after meeting Frank, and he generously offered to come stay with me and care for me. My rehab wouldn't be too bad, and he understood the process well; he'd had multiple surgeries on his knee, which had troubled him since his days as a college football player. It also helped that he's about twice my size and in great shape, so the physical demands wouldn't be a problem for him. I accepted his help gratefully, and it strengthened the growing bond between us.

Some months later, it was his turn to go under the knife, for another round of surgery on his knee. I'm a registered nurse, his devoted partner, and I'd received his caregiving, so it seemed logical that I'd return the favor, right? Not so fast. I had some real misgivings about my ability to care for him. I had taken care of my husband through many health crises, with numerous surgeries and hospitalizations, and he and I were both concerned about how this would impact our relationship. The recovery from a knee surgery is much more intensive and involves heavy medication. Though I can still make my way around a golf course, I didn't think I'd do well carting around a one-legged, half-conscious 220-pound man. I could put him at risk for re-injuring himself.

It wasn't an easy decision. I felt some obligation, and also some guilt, because he'd taken such good care of me. I didn't want him to feel abandoned. Frank recognized all these things, though, and he told me that he felt that having others take care of him until he could function on his own would protect our relationship. It was a big relief when he said he would be willing to recover in a rehab unit.

Have these conversations with your partner and don't let yourself be pushed around by the medical community and their biases. And don't over-promise about caregiving in a new relationship—it's a perfect recipe for burnout and resentment. There are always alternative plans. You just need to say, "I am not available to give this level of care."

Caregiver burnout

Caregiver burnout, also known as caregiver stress syndrome, is a state of exhaustion that can arise after a prolonged period of intense caregiving. It can involve physical, mental, and emotional symptoms, and can include depression, heart disease, dietary issues, and immune problems, among other complications. It typically arises when the caregiver puts their own health to the side in order to tend to their spouse's needs, whether after an injury or during sickness.

The risk for caregiver burnout has increased over the last few decades, in large part because medical science has advanced, providing more types of outpatient surgeries and treatments to help people stay alive and active longer. Our increased life spans are a wonderful effect of all these advancements, of course, but in order to avoid the downside, it's important to know your true capabilities as a caregiver. Even if your responsibilities don't put you at risk for full-blown caregiver burnout, there's still a chance of falling into bitterness and resentment if you become overextended. The effects can last well beyond the immediate situation.

Many of our clients, especially widows, are reluctant to get into new relationships, as they have taken care of sick husbands and don't want to be primary caregivers again. Well-meaning family members who have witnessed the years of sacrifice can unknowingly exacerbate this situation with statements such as, "Oh, Mom, are you sure you want to take the risk of another sick partner?" It is sad to think that fear of future caregiving could stop someone from seeking out a new and loving relationship, but we've seen it happen many times.

FRANK

My Aunt Claire had a loving and caring connection with her husband, Paul, for twenty years. Then he, at 84, had a stroke, and it became difficult for him to dress or get out of a chair. He was determined not to let anyone but Claire care for him, and even though I encouraged her to get outside help, she was determined to provide the care he needed.

Claire was a small lady, and Paul was six-foot-two and weighed more than 200 pounds. It wasn't long before she got to the point that even helping him out of his chair was too much for her. I watched her becoming increasingly frustrated and angry and finally even verbally abusive to him out of frustration. I urged her to look for professional help, but to no avail. The love between them had become a thing of the past, but she never acknowledged the need for a care facility or even someone who could come help in the home.

It broke my heart to see the change in such a wonderful person, but it taught me how important it is to plan for the future. As in my aunt's case, it has been our experience that men often avoid talking about assisted living or home care. It can be hard for them to confront their mortality, and many of them equate the need for help with weakness. As a result, they tend to avoid moving into a more supportive environment where there might be professional caregivers or even to discuss access to aids like wheelchairs, walkers, and so on. This misguided "independence" actually places a large burden on their families, increasing the chances of caregiver burnout at home. When entering into these conversations with a partner, understand how your joint feelings and decisions can have potentially serious consequences for those around you.

Senior care

Speaking of independence, the question of where to spend our final years is another big issue. Many of us would love to spend the rest of our lives in the comfort and familiarity of our homes, and many of us do. According to *The New England Journal of Medicine*, more than 50 percent of people are able to remain at home throughout their lives. However, end-of-life care and health complications often require us to move into assisted living facilities. There are many types, depending on the level and nature of the care required, and there can be widely differing opinions on when it's advisable to seek out these options. It can be a difficult, polarizing decision, so it's best to have this conversation early before there's a need or a crisis.

 # GLORIA

When my husband died, I wanted to know that I'd be in safe hands, so I purchased a condo in a senior living complex. When Frank and I got together, I knew I'd have to bring it up with him eventually. I was nervous, because I've seen a lot of my male clients protest about such places, and a lot of my friends have had pushback from their husbands when they've brought up the topic. I was surprised and pleased when he embraced the idea. We've since visited the place several times, and it always makes me laugh when he calls it a "summer camp for seniors."

If you find yourself or a loved one in need of the sort of care these facilities offer, try to focus on the many benefits they provide rather than solely on the perceived loss of independence. It can be a difficult adjustment, but it can make a big difference in quality of life. And it can provide your extended family with the reassurance that you're being well cared-for.

Medical power of attorney

If you become incapacitated, who do you want to make medical decisions on your behalf? The rules around this can vary from state to state and even from hospital to hospital, even if you're married, so if you don't take steps to designate someone, this could be left to chance. This is particularly true for same-sex couples, who are often subject to discrimination when it comes to such fundamental rights as hospital visitation. Gloria worked with the AIDS Health Project at San Francisco General Hospital in the nineties and recalls a number of very sad cases where same-sex partners were barred from participating in treatment, or even from just visiting their loved ones.

Instead of taking a risk regarding decisions about medical treatment, you can file paperwork to grant medical power of attorney to the designee of your choice. At some point in a developing relationship, reassess these arrangements. Perhaps it would make sense for a new partner to act on your behalf, or perhaps it would make more sense to have someone else hold that power. We decided not to make any changes to our situations. Gloria's children retain medical power of attorney for her, as Frank's stepdaughters do for him.

Issues with medications

Issues around prescription medications such as antidepressants, opioids, and anxiety medications can have a real impact on a developing relationship. It takes a lot of diligence and self-advocacy to make sure we're taking the right things, and only what's necessary, and when we don't put in the effort the result can often be that our meds are under-prescribed or over-prescribed. This can cause issues with mood regulation, to say nothing of the possible health effects.

One of our clients, Jim, a commercial airline pilot, told us that he and his partner Eleanor had decided to live together when he learned that she was on an antidepressant and on medications for high blood pressure, anxiety, and sleeping. She had been taking them for years and admitted to him that she was not sure why she was still taking them. Jim expressed his concerns, and she scheduled a re-assessment with her doctor. Together, they discovered that she didn't need some of the medications. Her doctor adjusted the other medications she was still taking. Jim and Eleanor moved in together and were comfortable and confident that her health and medications were assessed correctly.

This is another important area for open, honest conversations, but it can be tricky to figure out how and when to have this talk. There are concerns about privacy, and a newfound love might be reluctant to talk about the medications they are taking. We've heard clients say they were afraid that talking about their medication use would make them seem "weak" or "undesirable."

Another of our clients, Mary, a "wild child" of the sixties, takes this issue *very* seriously. She told us that before she gets too serious with anyone, she likes to visit them at home and use the master bathroom. While there she opens the medicine cabinet and takes pictures of all their meds so she can look them up later. Now, we're *not* advising you to follow her example! Instead, our recommendation is to approach the topic with understanding, patience, and empathy, creating a space for a supportive, open conversation about this serious issue.

FRANK

Infidelity

Infidelity is probably the number-one issue that causes many promising relationships to fail. In my first marriage, my wife was a graduate student and had an affair with her practicum supervisor. I had moved from Arizona to New York so that she could attend school and I was working to support us both. The betrayal would be devastating for anyone, but it was particularly painful for me, as my mother had had affairs, and I'd witnessed the damage it did to my father. I couldn't let the same pattern develop for me. She wanted us to go into counseling to save the marriage, but I couldn't. I didn't even allow her to explain her reasons. I just knew, given my family history, that I would never look at her the same way again.

Affairs are almost universally experienced as major crises, but reactions to the news are very specific to the individual. After the initial wave of emotion passes, some spouses see affairs as a way to work on latent issues that might not have surfaced otherwise. Other spouses withdraw and shut down, and still others may set out to have affairs of their own, figuring it's justified. Whatever the initial reactions might be, counseling is critical if a marriage is to survive.

That first marriage was not my only go-round with infidelity; it happened again, in a later marriage. I'd hoped that with maturity I would be able to give my wife the chance to explain and try to heal the relationship, but this was not to be the case, and our marriage collapsed. I did, however, have the wisdom to take some responsibility this time. I'd known early in our relationship that she'd had previous affairs, so I knew the potential was there all along.

It may seem obvious but be very cautious when considering a relationship with someone who has a record of infidelity. Past history is the greatest predictor of future behavior, after all. If you have a history of being attracted to cheaters, then you might need to take a step back and examine that. As we discussed in the early chapters, a big mismatch between what we say we want and what we're actually drawn to means it's time for a bit of self-examination. I failed to do this in my younger years, and I paid heavily for it.

Alcohol abuse

Alcohol is a potentially addictive drug that can seriously affect how the brain works and that causes changes in mood and awareness. According to *Harvard Health*, there is a serious rise in alcohol abuse by older adults. Their study reported that 20 percent of respondents drank alcohol four or more times a week, 27 percent reported having six or more drinks on at least one occasion, and seven percent reported alcohol-related blackouts. It is recommended that women have no more than one drink at a time and men no more than two. However, exceeding these recommendations is common practice, and we've heard countless complaints from our clients about alcohol use by their partners.

FRANK

Mike, a prominent contractor, sought out my advice when he became concerned about his partner's drinking. Susie, his girlfriend, was an artist who worked in their home studio. He told me he had noticed she was drinking wine every night, which to him was not entirely unusual, but she was also having drinks at lunch. At first, her behavior didn't seem to be much affected, so his concerns were only mild. But then, Susie's daughter approached him and voiced her own concerns about her mother's drinking. Mike started paying closer attention and he noticed how the empty wine bottles were piling up in the recycling. At the same time, he noticed that he was feeling more and more distant from Susie. "It's like she's not there anymore," he told me.

With my encouragement and support, he decided to talk to her and show his concern. Unfortunately, it did not go well. She got angry and said that she was tired of his "criticisms." She refused to come to a couple's session in my office and told him if he continued this criticism of her drinking, she was prepared to end the relationship. This extreme response really surprised Mike, but her reaction confirmed that he and their daughter had been right about her problematic relationship with alcohol. It was clear he had a real crisis on his hands. With Susie unwilling to admit she had a problem and seek out the required help, their relationship continued to deteriorate, and they eventually separated.

It is not unusual for someone who is abusing alcohol or other substances to react with denial, anger, or both, and this can be extremely difficult for loved ones who are looking to help. Modern thinking regards addiction as more of a health issue, rather than just a behavioral issue, and medical professionals and substance abuse counselors can assist on the road back to sobriety. But recovery depends on the patient's desire to get better, and sadly, many people like Susie would rather give up their relationships than face their addictions. So, if you think alcohol may be a problem in your relationship, we suggest addressing it earlier rather than later. Be aware that if it's a serious situation, you'll likely also need professional help, and it could be a long road ahead.

I was married to a successful hair salon owner at one point. As with Susie, it was common for her to have drinks in the evening, but then I noticed that she was drinking at lunch, too. I confronted her with my concerns and that led me to an understanding of just how reliant she was on alcohol. I came to realize how a person could be successful in their profession and still have serious addiction issues. Like many people whose loved ones are dealing with active addiction, I came to feel that to her, alcohol was more important than I was, and we eventually separated and divorced.

Dementia and Alzheimer's disease

This topic is a tough one. It's also a relatively recent development.

At the beginning of the twentieth century, life expectancy in the US was about 47 years. With the advances in medicine and improvements to our quality of life over the last century, we've extended the average lifespan by 30 years. Our medical advancements have led to amazing improvements in things like infant mortality, infectious diseases, and surgical procedures, but there is much about the aging brain and its associated cognitive issues that remain a mystery.

Cognitive impairment is a wide-ranging condition that can be temporary or severe, as in acute organic brain syndrome, which can be caused by an injury to the brain or by other disease factors. This syndrome can also be chronic, which we call dementia, and the most common type of dementia is Alzheimer's disease, which strikes one in nine Americans over the age of 65. The loss of memory and functionality can be heartbreaking and can create major challenges to a relationship.

As you and your partner approach and enter your sixties, it would be wise to take an inventory of risk factors and think about what a diagnosis might mean for your relationship. There is a genetic component to Alzheimer's, and information from a doctor or from genetic screening services (like 23 and Me) can determine if you're carrying any of these genetic markers. You can also find out a lot by looking at the family medical history. Did one or more of your parents or your partner's parents have Alzheimer's? If so, ask how this could affect the nature of your relationship, and whether you're up for the potential challenges.

One of our clients, Sam, a retired postal worker, found love after the death of a spouse with a fantastic woman, Brenda. He had enjoyed being married to Brenda for 15 years when she developed the early stages of Alzheimer's. He planned to see her through the stages of the disease, whatever it took. Another of our clients, Hank, a bartender, had been with his partner June for only two years when she was diagnosed with dementia. Unlike Sam, Hank recognized that he was not capable of taking care of June. Together they agreed to end the relationship. He felt bad but decided he would go about it in the most responsible and caring way possible. He even spoke to her children as he was making his decision so he could be sure they were there and ready to give her support.

These are tough choices that must be faced honestly and directly by both partners. We have seen countless situations like these among our clients, and things always go much better when people make conscious, careful decisions ahead of time, rather than waiting to be surprised.

Long-distance relationships

There are many situations that can keep committed couples from being together regularly. We have couples in our practices who live long distances from each other, whether because of their jobs, finances, or caregiving responsibilities with elderly parents. If you are in this situation, take heart. Meeting online sometimes means that you might each live in different states or even different countries. It is not easy, but in our practices, we have worked with individuals who experienced this challenge and made it work.

FRANK

Sean, a sixty-three-year-old engineer, had been divorced for two years before he met Juanita at his firm in the southwestern US. She was from Mexico and while they were dating, she had to go back to take care of her ailing mother and father. Sean came to counseling to see how he could keep the relationship together in her absence. I told him that the research I had participated in regarding long-distance relationships indicated that as long as the partners remained loyal and did not date other people, the connection could be maintained.

He was encouraged to hear of a study I'd participated in while at Columbia University that looked at "commuter couples" who were split between New York City and Washington, DC. The research revealed some truth behind the old adage that "absence makes the heart grow fonder." The study's participants reported that the time away made them miss their partner and made the time together special. The positive outcomes for these couples were encouraging for Sean and Juanita, and they worked out a plan to maintain their relationship while she was away. It worked, and they reunited two years later.

There are other circumstances besides physical separation that can delay togetherness, as with Judy and Chris. We met Judy while she was caring for her ailing husband Charlie, who had been bed-bound with terminal cancer for a year. While caring for him, she found herself drawn to his friend Chris, a single divorced man who had also been helping with Charlie's care. Eventually, they fell in love with each other, but Judy was in distress because she felt that she could not abandon her husband or his care.

It was very difficult for Judy and Chris but they both wanted to honor their commitment to Charlie and his desire to end his life at home. A few months after he passed away, they married and were glad that they honored Charlie's wishes and supported his final months at home. The time that they waited to be together only increased their trust and commitment to one another.

Wrap-up

As these stories reveal, even committed and promising relationships have their ups and downs. Life poses many challenges. In the next chapter, we will take a close look at the topic of grief and how past losses can affect the present and the future. We will explore the role of grief in a person's ability to move on to new experiences and be open to love.

Journal questions

If you're in a committed relationship, think about how you might handle some of the challenges discussed in this chapter.

Practice conversation

How might you ask a future partner—in a respectful but direct way—about their health or end-of-life care? Write out a few sentences.

"MAYBE YOU'RE NOT READY TO START DATING AGAIN."

CHAPTER NINE

Bereavement and Grief

In Chapter Seven, we took a close look at "almost experiences," relationships that don't quite go the distance and can leave us nursing a broken heart. In this chapter, we'll take a close look at the aftermath of the other big reason we seniors find ourselves alone: death of a partner. The two types of loss share some similarities, but there are significant differences between them, and those of us who are widows and widowers can benefit from an awareness of the process of loss and the long-term effects it can have. Our past losses can and will impact how we respond to our current losses, and unprocessed grief can reach down through many years to trigger us, resulting in some surprising and difficult responses to what might seem like minor occurrences. We all have places of pain we visit on occasion; the difference here is how long we stay there, and how prepared we are when they arise.

 # GLORIA

I lost my son many years ago, and Frank lost his father when he was 15. Through the years, we have both processed these significant losses through therapy, education, and peer and family support. After what we went through, Frank and I realized three things: we would live, we would not go crazy, and we could and would be happy again. By the time we met each other, we were both aware of our needs. We recognized the impermanence of life and we both knew we wanted a companion. (Because of this, we were prepared to move into a serious relationship very quickly, within a matter of weeks. It was very exciting and quite magical, and it still is.)

By middle age, most of us have experienced the pain of losing a beloved friend or family member. We've been through the shock and grief, and we've developed coping skills to get us through and keep us moving forward. The result of these processes is wisdom, which can be a huge help when embarking on a new relationship as well.

Assess your readiness

If you've lost someone, it can be hard to know how much it might impact the ability to find a new partner. Here are four simple grief assessment questions to help determine where you are in the process, and whether or not you're ready to date with an open heart and an open mind:

- Does a partner's absence dominate your daily activities?
- Are intrusive thoughts of a past partner still impeding your progress?
- Do you avoid going to places or doing things you did with a partner?
- How comfortable are you talking about the loss?

Does a partner's absence dominate your daily activities?

How much energy do you put into thinking or talking about the loss of a partner? The death of a partner tops the list of the most stressful life experiences, and it can be particularly painful when it's unexpected, as with an auto accident or an unforeseen heart attack. What follows is a difficult grieving process.

In the late 1960s, the Swiss-American psychiatrist Elisabeth Kübler-Ross defined five aspects of grief: denial, anger, bargaining, depression, and acceptance. The process she described in her book *On Death and Dying* has seen widespread acceptance, but it is often interpreted as a linear series of stages. This was not her intention, however. In her work with terminal patients, she observed various routes through these five stages, including several patients who skipped one or more altogether, and other patients who would cycle through certain stages repeatedly. The ideal end result is acceptance, but everyone takes different pathways to get there.

The key is to keep moving toward healing. As psychologists, we get concerned when somebody stalls out before reaching acceptance. We've had clients who, even after years in some cases, spend an inordinate amount of time talking about a partner who has died or left them. Sometimes the deceased can command so much attention it even seems as if they're still in the picture.

Our client Mabel came in one day, very excited about going hiking with a man she had met at the produce counter of the grocery store. They got to chatting and discovered they were both buying items for an upcoming hike, so they planned to hike together. When she came back the following week, she said that the date had been a bust. He'd spent the entire time talking about his wife, who'd died the previous year. She felt bad for him, but it was certainly not the date she'd been hoping for. "It was like she was on the hike with us," Mabel said.

About one in ten bereaved individuals suffers from prolonged grief disorder, which the World Health Organization defines as a "persistent and pervasive grief response characterized by longing for the deceased or persistent preoccupation with the deceased accompanied by intense emotional pain ... [which] has persisted for an atypically long period of time following the loss ... and clearly exceeds expected social, cultural, or religious norms for the individual's culture and context." The "atypically long period of time" is generally defined as six months, although, again, social, cultural, and religious norms are considered. In the US, six months is a fairly useful measurement for when we therapists would hope to see the intensity of grief diminishing.

If you can identify with the diagnosis above, we urge you to seek counseling as soon as possible. If you have questions about how far removed you are from a divorce or the death of a partner, take a closer look at your grief and have an honest conversation with yourself about where you are in the process. If you remain in disbelief about what happened, you could still be in early grief. It's normal for people to occasionally feel anger long after a divorce, but if you find that your thoughts about the split are dominated by angry feelings, you're still working through that grief. Do you hope your ex will change their mind and come back, or do you often feel depressed about the loss? Give yourself time to move through the feelings of loss, and lean on a therapist, trusted friends, and support groups to keep from getting stuck.

Are intrusive thoughts of a past partner
still impeding your progress?

In early grief and loss, it is not unusual to think that you see or hear the voices of people who have died or left. According to Mary-Frances O'Connor, author of *The Grieving Brain*, this is because the brain is trained to look for the familiar. Thinking you see a loved one across a crowded room is not unusual. What can be problematic is if you become disturbed and experience persistent anxiety related to the absent person.

A note to readers: If the loss you suffered was abrupt or traumatic, as in the distressing case that follows, you may have some strong brain imprints that need attention. That said, please read this vignette only if you are comfortable. If you're not ready, you can choose to wait and come back to it later.

FRANK

When Walter's wife committed suicide, he was the one who found her hanging from the rafters. Afterward, for many months, powerful images of his wife's death would strike him at what he called "strange times." Once he felt he was ready to date, he found a dating app and met Pat, with whom he thought he would be compatible. She, like him, was a professional and in her spare time played tennis. They talked on the telephone and then shifted to video calls and were looking forward to meeting each other in person. They made a date to play tennis and had a wonderful time, after which they sat down for a drink. As they talked, he was overcome with feelings of anxiety and guilt. Suddenly, he blurted out, "My wife committed suicide. And I found her, and I had to cut her down." He then began to weep.

The incident was so disturbing that when Walter came to therapy, he was in severe distress. He was anxious and apprehensive, and terrified of setting up another online date. I reassured him that I could help him address the horrible memories of the moments around his wife's death. His flashbacks were not unusual given the circumstances.

I successfully treated him with Eye Movement Desensitization and Reprogramming (EMDR) therapy, a desensitization technique developed by psychologist Francine Shapiro and disseminated in the 1990s. In EMDR, the patient visualizes the traumatic event while also experiencing bilateral brain stimulation, often by moving the eyes rapidly back and forth. Physical stimuli, such as bilateral tapping or mild electrical currents, can also work. Over time, the bilateral stimulation diminishes the intensity of the targeted experience, and it loses its charge.

After a few sessions, Walter's flashbacks began to subside, and after only a few months, he was able to resume dating without fear. Severe trauma like his is not very common, fortunately, but if you are experiencing repercussions from something similarly powerful, please consider seeking out EMDR or another desensitization therapy. There are many trained providers and these techniques have helped millions of people since Shapiro's discovery.

Do you avoid going to places or doing things you did with a partner?

If you can't go to your favorite restaurant, movie theater, or bar because you are afraid you will see your ex, you may need to first talk it out with a friend or therapist. We have found desensitization therapy helpful in this situation as well. In this case, it is a simple technique where you gradually expose yourself to the event or place until it becomes more comfortable. (You can find out more about this process through the internet.)

Remember to be kind to yourself. And don't try to force yourself to do things you don't want to do. It is not unusual for people who have had a loss to avoid places or people that have been a part of their life with a past partner. This might not seem like a big deal if it's just a matter of avoiding the memories in a certain restaurant across town. But we have seen clients whose lives have been so completely disrupted that they couldn't enjoy their daily activities.

FRANK

Remember the story of my Aunt Claire, who experienced caregiver burnout while caring for my Uncle Paul after his stroke? Sadly, the story did not get better after his death. A widow now, Claire withdrew, and stopped several activities she had previously loved. She had once been quite a chef, but she stopped cooking and settled for take-out burgers several nights a week. She had been known for planning and hosting birthday parties for everyone in the family, but she lost interest in those as well. I tried to see her several times, but she would just say, "Oh, honey, don't bother with me. I'm just fine, and you have so many people to help." I did have a busy practice, but she was the one person I wanted to help the most. I did what I could to urge her to seek support, but my suggestions were met with as much success as my suggestions about Uncle Paul's care when he was alive.

It was very sad for me to witness my beloved aunt spending her days isolated and alone when I knew that there were alternatives to that scenario. She lived for another ten years, and she was in good health. I still wonder what opportunities might have come her way had she been able to connect with more people and stay engaged with the things she'd once loved.

GLORIA

My husband Phil and I owned a seaside house in California for more than 20 years. We spent many weekends and vacations there with our kids and grandkids and filled the house with wonderful memories. We built friendships in the surrounding community and played countless games on the nearby golf courses, which are some of the world's best. All ten of my grandchildren learned to golf there, and I was a part of the women's golf group. We walked on the beach, ate at the nearby restaurants, and attended local events, where we came to feel like locals. It was really our special place.

After Phil died, I could not bring myself to go back. The idea of returning to that house totally depressed me. Two months later I sold it and never went there again. I even asked my three daughters to clean out the house. They very kindly packed everything up, dividing the furniture amongst the family and putting the kitchen items and art into storage. That was three years ago, and I have yet to pull anything out of the storage unit. Frank and I are now renovating a house, and although I had planned on getting everything out of storage for our new place, I'm having second thoughts. I'm not sure that I want the reminders.

I still can't bring myself to go back to that charming town, even when my friends invite me for weekend golfing getaways. My granddaughter and her boyfriend recently spent the weekend in the area and when she told me she went by the house, I experienced some real discomfort just at the mention of it. I've been invited to a golf tournament this coming fall, and I'd like to be able to go. Maybe I will head down for a day trip beforehand to see how it feels. After three years, I think I am probably ready.

How comfortable are you talking about the loss?

Being able to tell the story of a loss is important. Individual therapy and support groups are great places for this. Trusted friends or family members can also be a huge support. When Gloria was on the faculty of a prestigious university, her friend, another professor, used to say, "If you had three good friends or relatives that you could tell everything, you wouldn't need a therapist."

There are many people, however, who aren't comfortable talking about death, or even divorce. Amid your struggles, then, some relatives or old friends might be avoiding you. Yet you can also make new friends who understand and have suffered similar losses. Welcome the new friends but don't give up on the others. When you are more settled, they might reappear. Even if they aren't comfortable providing grief support, they may have something else to offer, even if it's just distraction through a movie outing or a game of tennis.

Identify a few key friends or relatives who provide a safe place to talk about your feelings and keep them close. Triggered grief can arise without warning, and you never know when you might need to make a call. We like to say that when you are bored with your own story or that of your ex's escapades, you will know you have done the work of grieving.

Wrap-up

If you're struggling to progress through unresolved grief and loss, we urge you to find a therapist or a local support group. If you are not sure where to get help, contact the local information and referral service in your city. There are many online resources as well. For example, the website of The Center for Prolonged Grief at Columbia University is filled with useful information and includes directories of trained grief therapists. You can also get help by visiting the website of our foundation, Open to Hope, where you will find thousands of articles, podcasts, and videos, all aimed at helping find hope after loss.

Remember that every cloud has a silver lining. In the next chapter we will talk about a much-neglected topic, which is posttraumatic growth. We believe that we can each transform our pain and come to find personal growth through our loss.

Journal questions

Consider some of the questions we posed in this chapter, and write down your answers:

- Does a partner's absence dominate your daily activities?
- Are intrusive thoughts of a past partner still impeding your progress?
- Do you avoid going to places you used to visit or doing the things you did with a partner?
- How comfortable are you talking about the loss?

"I WANT TO HURRY UP AND MAKE SOME MEMORIES BEFORE I START FORGETTING THINGS."

" I SENSED THERE WAS MAGIC WHEN
SHE LET ME PARK IN HER DRIVEWAY."

CHAPTER TEN

Posttraumatic Growth

Who hasn't heard the old adage, "What doesn't kill us makes us stronger"? Adversity and growth often go hand-in-hand. Put differently, to truly know the light, we must understand the darkness, and to know the full scope of happiness, we must know sadness.

The American Psychological Association defines resilience as "successfully adapting to difficult or challenging life experiences." As therapists, we consider this to be an acceptable outcome when we're treating someone who has suffered loss, but our real goal goes one step further. The ideal outcome is posttraumatic *growth*, adapting to challenges and coming away not just surviving but thriving, with the mindset that challenging times can be opportunities for growth. With posttraumatic growth, we emerge from adversity even better than before, with new understanding, having learned from our experiences. We're not just resilient, but brilliant—the star of our own story.

We have both experienced posttraumatic growth many times

over, and we have been inspired by our clients and family members who have suffered great adversity, processed it, and moved on to not only experience productive and happy lives, but also to use their experiences to benefit others.

Posttraumatic growth doesn't happen overnight. In fact, for those in the throes of a traumatic loss, the idea of posttraumatic growth can even be distasteful. Gloria, a bereaved parent herself, would *never* suggest to a recently bereaved parent that they might grow through their experience. Most of us in early loss are just trying to get through the day. Wherever you are in the process, an understanding of posttraumatic growth will be one more tool to measure how far you've come and to gauge your readiness for dating.

FRANK

I was surprised one morning to receive a message from my childhood friend, Justin. He said that he would be in town for a few days and would like to talk, as he had not been able to sleep properly for more than a year. I'd last heard from Justin several years prior, right about when we turned 70. He was living and working in the Los Angeles area and had the energy of a man half his age, which is how I'd always known him. As a kid, he was very athletic, a free spirit, and very popular with girls. After graduation, he moved to

California, and every time we checked in it seemed like he was living a full, vibrant life.

I called him back and told him he could stay at the small, detached building on my property that doubled as my office and a guest house. The man who appeared looked little like the Justin whom I'd known in our younger years. He had aged and was nervous, agitated, and frustrated. After a big hug, we settled in, and he told me what he'd been going through for the previous year. The woman he'd been dating, Georgia, a heavy drinker, had died suddenly from a fall, and he was the one who found her. He'd arrived at her front door and could hear her dog going crazy behind it. When Georgia didn't answer his knocks, he forced his way into the apartment, where he discovered the accident.

For the next six weeks, Justin was a "person of interest" in the case until the medical examiners finally ruled the death an accident. He'd been exonerated, but he could not get the image of her lying on the floor out of his head. He became lonely and very angry. At the funeral, Georgia's mother, as well as her brother, whom he'd come to know, were very cold and distant toward him, and he could tell they felt he might have been involved in her death. He liked them and their suspicions made him feel awful. He even told me that her mother, at the funeral, had been staring at him like he was a murderer, and he could not get her face out of his mind.

I suggested that he see a therapist I knew who specialized in trauma, which he did. We continued to have long talks on the phone, and after six months of therapy, I saw the beginnings of posttraumatic growth within my friend. He was sleeping better, taking regular walks on the beach, and reviewing his gratitude list, as his therapist had suggested. He told me that even with the loss of Georgia, he was able to be grateful for the good times they had. The therapist had also suggested that Justin write a letter to Georgia's mother and brother, expressing his sorrow over losing Georgia and his relationship with them as well. They did not respond, but it still gave him a sense of closure.

He told me that he was so grateful we had reconnected. I promised I'd keep in regular contact, and he said he was contacting other old friends and sharing his loss and healing with them. I'd never known Justin to be very spiritual, but he told me that he was working on his forgiveness toward the police, her family, and toward Georgia herself. This practice was working and his energy for life and adventure were returning. I told him that I was proud of him for turning his life around after the trauma he'd been through. It can take a while to attain posttraumatic growth, but I had faith in Justin's ability to grow through his loss; once he dedicated himself to his healing, the growth was there for all to see.

The five areas of posttraumatic growth

By the time we reach senior status, the vast majority of us have experienced some type of loss or some other type of adversity. How did you respond? What was it like to go through that, and how did you feel afterward? Perhaps you've already experienced some posttraumatic growth.

Richard Tedeschi and Lawrence Calhoun, the psychologists

whose work brought this phenomenon to light, identify five areas of posttraumatic growth:

1. Greater appreciation for life
2. Formation of stronger relationships
3. Discovery of new possibilities
4. Growth of personal strength
5. Spiritual growth

Take a look and see if you can find some areas where you have grown. Note the areas where you would like to continue to develop.

FRANK

1. Greater appreciation for life

When our lives take a turn, we often find a greater capacity for feeling and expressing gratitude. When I was in high school, I was a very quiet kid, whom few people knew but for a few close friends. When I was 15, my father died of a heart attack. I was the first in my school to lose a parent and many teachers and classmates reached out to me in my loss. I was heartbroken, but the school rallied around me. That year they created a new position on the student council for me called the Chaplain, voted for me for Best Dancer, and elected me Prom King. I went from a relative unknown to a celebrity in one year. As the student body's chaplain, I opened all the assemblies with a prayer. I never felt so loved. I really grew up that year and developed an appreciation for all the connections that my father's death had brought my way. I missed my father but grew in my grief to accept the attention and accept the gift my father's death had given me. I know that this support was a major factor in choosing the field of psychology, where I could give back the love and support that I received around my father's death.

2. Formation of stronger relationships

Loss can give one the clear realization that we are all vulnerable and can lead us to become less critical and more empathetic regarding the losses of others. Positive community and peer support and lifetime friendships often develop in the aftermath of such losses.

Our friend Carl was a rather formal and rule-oriented member of the highway patrol when he was called to an accident where a child had died. In the cruelest of coincidences, it turned out that the child was his, and the driver was his ex-wife, who was drunk. This was her third DWI, and she went to prison.

Carl was devastated but over time and through his volunteer work with Mothers Against Drunk Driving (MADD), he softened, becoming more empathetic and loving. Over time, he has developed strong bonds and relationships by helping thousands of people impacted by impaired drivers.

Gloria's three daughters present another example; the death of their brother caused them to develop strong family bonds. In fact, all three of the girls work with one another to support the foundation that grew out of their brother's death.

3. Discovery of new possibilities

Being shaken out of the life you thought you were going to lead can change not only your perspective but can also move you into new areas of interest. Our friend Michelle thought that she and her husband would work as physical trainers and open their own gym, but fate took another direction. While her husband was out jogging, he had a fatal heart attack. As a young widow, Michelle looked to others for help and support but felt that there was something missing. Rather than giving up, she rallied and started her own support organization for spousal loss. She decided that she should get widowed people together, and she organized the first Soaring Spirits International conference, funding the whole thing with her personal credit card. Soaring Spirits has since become the premier organization for support after the loss of a spouse, helping thousands of people yearly.

Candace Lightner founded Mothers Against Drunk Driving (MADD) as a result of the death of her thirteen-year-old daughter, Cari, at the hands of a repeat-offending drunk driver. At the time, drunk drivers were only given a sentence of a few months. Candace spent three years after Cari's death working to change legislation in Washington D.C. Her tragedy moved her to build a world-changing support and advocacy organization, whose mission is in full swing more than 40 years after the event that inspired its creation.

4. Growth of personal strength

In Tedeschi and Calhoun's research, they found that those who have suffered loss often have more resilience and an increased ability to bounce back. The stress of loss leads many to become more self-reliant, authentic, and humble. When we think about personal strength, we think of Victor Frankl's book *Man's Search for Meaning*, an account of his time in a concentration camp during WWII. In 1942, Frankl and his family were sent to the Theresienstadt Concentration Camp, where his father died of starvation and pneumonia. Two years later, Frankl and the surviving members of his family were transported to Auschwitz, where his mother and brother were murdered in the gas chambers. After his release from the camp, Frankl went on to have a full life and as a psychiatrist. He developed a method called logotherapy, which focuses on the search for life's meaning. He helped thousands of patients with depression, substance abuse, anxiety, and various other problems.

5. Spiritual growth

Following traumatic times, Tedeschi and Calhoun found that subjects in their study emerged with deeper, more meaningful beliefs and life philosophies. Such was the case for me in 1983, when my seventeen-year-old son Scott died in an automobile crash, an event that shook my belief system. I was raised in the Mormon church and had accepted its teachings without question, but now I found myself asking where God was and why God would let such a thing happen. I studied and searched but found no answers, and eventually lost my faith.

One day I met a pastor, and we fell into conversation. I expressed my love and admiration for the kind people I'd met through church but complained about the unhelpful theology. "Gloria," he said, "the people *are* the church. They are God's emissaries on Earth." That changed my whole perspective, and I came to realize how important and life-changing the church had really been for me. And when my husband of 60 years died of a staph infection following back surgery, I didn't feel that God had abandoned me. Instead, I recognized the blessings of my family, friends, and the strangers who showed up for me in the name of God.

Posttraumatic love

We believe that having known love and loss and then finding another soulmate can lift people beyond resilience. We have found that almost all of our friends and clients who have progressed through loss to dating have grown in areas that they themselves had not foreseen. We don't think this is a coincidence; in fact, we believe that love and human connection around life's trials are some of the major catalysts of posttraumatic growth. We thus talk to our clients about "posttraumatic love": a particularly resilient, mature type of love you only get to enjoy after walking through a fire or two. We've experienced it ourselves, and we've seen it among our clients and many of our friends. (Perhaps now it's your turn.)

 # GLORIA

Carter, a successful psychologist with a private practice, came into my office feeling very frustrated and agitated. He had a great smile but was clearly very depressed. He started our conversation by telling me that his wife had "really screwed him over."

He and his wife Harper, also a psychologist, had a very successful private practice, which they ran out of their large home. They had offices in separate wings and were known for running innovative couples' groups. While Carter had never been married, Harper had a teenage daughter from a previous marriage to whom Carter had become very close. He described her as a "lovely girl, bright and beautiful." It was the family he never had.

They were the picture of happiness until Harper had an affair with a female client, a local lawyer. Carter felt betrayed but also very confused, as Harper had never expressed interest in women before. Realizing her mistake, Harper tried to end the affair. Her spurned, angry client, however, decided to turn her in to the licensure board. Harper was facing the probable loss of her license, which would jeopardize not only their business, but also their ability to keep their home. After being reported, Harper had gone to Carter, begging him to stay and support her. She insisted she had done nothing wrong. To her it was a consensual relationship that had just shown poor judgment, a misguided reaction to her parents' recent deaths. She felt that the professional board was being unfair in threatening to take her license.

Carter was shocked and saddened at her lack of remorse. For him, that meant the end. He moved out of the house and put it on the market. Summarizing his losses, he told me, "I lost my professional partner, my marriage partner, my stepdaughter, my home, my business location, and my reputation all at once." As a therapist, he realized the multiple traumatic aspects of the situation, and he understood what this type of trauma can do to people. He knew he had a lot of work ahead to get through it. I referred him to a specialist and invited him to reach out to me anytime.

A year later he came back to see me. The first thing I noticed was that he looked good and had lost weight. With the proceeds from the home sale, he had gotten himself a new place and restarted his practice. He'd found that his reputation had not taken the blow he feared. People had stopped asking about Harper and he was deeply appreciative for how far he'd come. He'd reconnected with some old friends who'd fallen by the wayside in the course of his relationship with Harper and he'd joined a men's spiritual group, on which he'd come to depend for support and guidance. They met weekly, and he'd never missed a session. Even better, his relationship with his stepdaughter had survived. He didn't see her as often as he would have liked, but their bond remained intact and strong. Carter told me that he wasn't afraid or anxious about future losses because he'd learned that he's strong enough to not only survive but to prosper.

He lit up the most, though, when talking about the woman he

was dating. It was a new relationship. He'd spent most of the previous year recovering from what had happened with Harper and getting clear about what kind of relationship he wanted, and what he didn't want. Knowing how those early stages of a relationship can be intoxicating, I usually listen to such stories with some skepticism, but Carter and his new love had made it through the forming stage (see Chapter Seven) and were now putting in the work of joining their lives. They were discovering new compatibility at every turn and planning all sorts of adventures together. He told me that his relationship with Harper—and all the relationships he'd had prior—had prepared him to show up for this one in a whole new way. He said he felt more like himself than ever before, and he felt an excitement for life he never could have imagined a year earlier.

Growth and love

At this age, who among us hasn't been through a dark time or two? Loss and heartbreak are factors in life, part of the universal balance that makes falling in love so wondrous. The only way to avoid the pain is also to avoid the joy—to stay home and keep to yourself, where nobody can find you. If you've stuck with us this far, though, that's clearly not for you. You might be at the very end of one relationship or the very beginning of the next. You might be right in between. You might not even know exactly where you are! Wherever that is, though, you're wiser, more self-aware, and more capable than you were on your last go-round, and your spirit of curiosity and openness will put you in an even better place tomorrow than the one you're in today.

Maybe you've still got a little work to do, and that's okay. In this chapter, we've listed a number of ways to find support and community as you continue to do that work, such as individual and group therapy, reaching out to close friends, finding support groups, and exploring religious or spiritual organizations. Spending time in nature, meditation, and exercise are other ways to bolster mental and physical well-being, promote healing, and keep your mind moving into a healthy, fulfilling future. Creating space for self-examination, whether through therapy or by setting aside quiet spaces and deliberate times, will promote better self-awareness and lead you to make the best choices possible.

Whatever you've been through, wherever you are, we've found that openness to love and perseverance can lead you to "The One," just as it did for us. Keep at it and know that everything you've been through has brought you to this unique point in life. We believe that the last, best love of your life is out there, waiting for you!

"THE BOTTOM LINE IS WE RESPECT EACH OTHER'S STYLE."

The Five Basic Rules of Dating

Stepping into the dating world is a big growth step. You might be just preparing to take the plunge, or you might be a seasoned veteran who's looking for ways to do it better. You might be at the beginning of a new and exciting relationship. Wherever you are, we've given you a lot to think about and do as you prepare to take the next steps. Next, just take a step back and give yourself a great big pat on the back.

One of our favorite quotations is from the movie *Auntie Mame*. Mame (played by Rosalind Russell) declares, "Life is a banquet and most poor suckers are starving to death." Like Mame, you're not interested in being one of those poor suckers. You're embracing life, challenging yourself to get out there and build new relationships. You've rejected stagnation and are committed to a future of growth and love.

We've covered a lot of ground in this book, beginning with preparations for dating. From there we moved through the ins and outs of meeting someone and covered the wild world of online dating. We took you through those early dates and into the four stages of a committed relationship, and then we talked about what happens when things don't quite go according to plan. It's a lot to remember, but this information will be here for reference as you progress through your dating adventure.

Finally, we'd like to leave you with our five basic rules of dating.

1. Don't give up

One of our clients went on fifty first dates. It might take a little while to find the love you're looking for. There could be some disappointing, lonely times along the way. But someone is out there. Just keep at it. Take it from us—it can be well worth it!

2. Keep making space in your life

Don't expect someone to just fall out of the sky while you're going about your business. Be active. Find a buddy or two to support you and put in the time and energy to do this right. As with any project, the more you put into it, the more you get back.

3. Go to where the action is

If you're an active person with a busy social life and lots of opportunities to meet people, keep at it. If not, then look for singles groups or other activities or communities where people are looking and open to love. There are millions of singles online, too; decide what works, and don't be shy about putting yourself out there.

4. Grow through setbacks

It isn't always going to be a great time. Approach each date, each person as an opportunity to learn a little more about yourself and what you're looking for. Be aware of your historical patterns and keep striving for what you know will be good for you.

5. Have fun!

You're at a sprawling, marvelous banquet. Even if you don't find the love of your life right away, take the time to appreciate all the people, places, and adventures. You could make some great friends along the way and collect a stack of stories to make your grandkids blush. It's your turn!

We are thrilled to have had the opportunity to write this book together. We hope that you have enjoyed both the male and female perspectives we brought to the project, and we hope we've inspired you to be open to love.

— Dr. Gloria Horsley and Dr. Frank Powers

Journal questions

How will you put what you've learned about dating and relationships into practice? Ask one more time, "What am I waiting for?"

Acknowledgments

Creating a book is a collaborative endeavor, and our gratitude extends to the many individuals whose contributions and support have made this one possible.

First and foremost, our families, friends, and clients deserve our heartfelt thanks. Their stories, experiences, and unwavering belief in us have been the bedrock upon which this book stands. To Gloria's daughters, Heidi, Rebecca, and Heather, and her sons-in-law John, Markus, and Carl, along with our grandchildren, step-grandchildren, and extended family, your love and encouragement have been our driving force.

We'd like to express our appreciation to those who guided and advised us throughout the writing process. Cynthia Morris, Ben Leroy, Jason Buchholz, and Nicki Van De Car, your insights helped shape this book into its final form.

Dr. Ken Druck, thank you for introducing us to the seasoned relationship writers Linda and Charlie Bloom, who provided invaluable encouragement and support.

We're indebted to Mariah Swift and Esther Fedorkevich at Fedd

Agency for taking on our project, as well as Ash Abraham for her meticulous editing and Mackenna Cotten for fabulous cover design. Our friend Patty McGuigan, thank you for your support and for sharing your valuable contacts, including the talented cartoonist, John Klossner.

Jill Colucci, your musical talents added a unique dimension to our project, and we're grateful for your contribution.

Meghan Johnson, Kristy Chan, and the rest of the team at Trifecta PR, thank you for believing in this book and supporting us in getting our message out in the world. And us on camera!

Our team at Open to Hope has been an invaluable source of support. Chris Gamble, Greg Vaughn, Neil Chethik, John Rampton, Angela Rampton, and the entire Open to Hope team, your dedication has been instrumental in bringing this book to fruition.

Sandra Wilken, thank you for sharing your online dating experiences, providing us with valuable insights into the ever-evolving world of virtual connections.

Rick Haskins, your wisdom from the media and marketing world has been a guiding light, and your ongoing advice has been invaluable. Thanks for being the best manager there ever was.

Lastly, we want to express our gratitude to the world of online dating. Without Silver Singles, our paths would never have crossed, and the "Dating Doctors" might have remained just a distant dream.

With profound thanks,
Dr. Frank and Dr. Gloria Horsley
AKA The Dating Doctors